# you and your handwriting

Your personality is revealed in every stroke of your handwriting. Here, the scientific study of handwriting analysis is explained clearly and simply for the layman.

Learn how to use this practical guide and develop new understanding of yourself and those around you.

Including revealing insights into the personalities of such people as

FRANK SINATRA
ELEANOR ROOSEVELT
MARY MARTIN
ELIZABETH TAYLOR

FIDEL CASTRO
RICHARD BURTON
NIKITA KHRUSHCHEV
CHARLES DE GAULLE

# you and your

# handwriting

by Muriel Stafford

**WILDSIDE PRESS**

© *Copyright 1963, by Muriel Stafford*

*All rights reserved*

# contents

*Introduction* . . . . . . . . *11*
"Graphologie." How personality and character were discovered to be apparent in handwriting. Development as a psychological diagnostic tool, starting with the research of the two Parisian monks who also gave the subject its name.

*1. Your Self-Image* . . . . . *19*
How you disclose self-evaluation as you write capital I . . . Teen-age problems . . . Capabilities, talents, complexes . . . Illustrated by writings of J. Edgar Hoover, Boris Karloff, Thornton Wilder. Case histories.

*2. You as an Entity* . . . . . *30*
Appraising a handwriting as a whole . . . speed and legibility . . . development of individuality . . . simplification vs. elaboration . . . Illus-

*trated by handwritings of President J. F. Kennedy, Celia Sanchez, Jayne Mansfield, Alfred Adler.*


*3. Invisible Borders . . . . 39*
*How margins stress introversion, extroversion, formality, informality, escapism, reserve, loquaciousness, extravagance, and so on.*


*4. So Leans Your Heart . . . 48*
*How emotional release vs. sublimation of emotion is revealed in the slant of letters. Changes in slant over a period of years; also changes due to temporary conditions or state of mind. Illustrated by the handwritings of Elizabeth Taylor (ages 12 and 18), Perry Como, Premier Nehru, Victor Borge, Cordell Hull, Richard Burton, and others. Case histories.*


*5. Emotional Impact . . . . 60*
*How forceful pen pressure reflects strength of will, self-assertion, materialistic tendencies, desire to dominate, and/or sensuality. Connotations of light pen pressure including compliance, responsiveness, and/or idealism. Examples: Greer Garson, Duchess of Windsor, Bill Cullen, Gypsy Rose Lee versus the handwriting of a nun. Case histories. Chart indicating the significance of pen pressure as affected by letter slant.*

## 6. Your Disposition and Temperament . . . . . 70
How the shape of connective strokes (rounded, pointed, garlanded, or thready) denotes disposition, talents and personality traits. Handwritings of Dag Hammarskjold, Premier Adenauer, Sister Mary Rosa, Tony Armstrong-Jones, Jimmy Durante. Case histories.

## 7. Your Libido . . . . . . . 79
How the shape and size of lower loops discloses complexes and reveals sexual and materialistic urges. Idealistic aspirations of upper loops. Handwritings of Bob Hope, James Mason, Conrad Hilton, Debbie Reynolds. Case histories. Chart showing 28 variations of loops with significance of each.

## 8. Social Consciousness . . . 89
Social awareness vs. egoistic, mental or spiritual absorption as denoted by the middle zone. Handwritings of Lily Pons, President de Gaulle, Kate Smith, Warren Hull, President Eisenhower, Mrs. Roosevelt, Tito. Case histories.

## 9. Your State of Mind, Health and Nerves . . . . . . . 100
How the psychological and physical condition of a writer becomes apparent in the invisible

*"baseline" beneath the lines of writing. Case histories.*

## 10. *Approach and Conclusion* . *106*
*The significance of beginning and ending strokes of a word. Ways that maturity, intelligence, and various character traits are expressed. Case histories.*

## 11. *Headlining of Personality* . *113*
*How capital letters highlight a writer's personality and talents. Examples: Lily Pons, Frank Sinatra. Twenty-one variations of M, each by a celebrity.*

## 12. *Eloquent Strokes* . . . . *124*
*How varied traits may be disclosed or emphasized by t-bars, i-dots, and certain specific letters. Illustrative examples including handwritings of Thomas E. Dewey and Clare Booth Luce.*

## 13. *Vocational Aptitudes* . . . *133*
*The development of handwriting as aptitudes and talents. How handwriting reveals aptitude for various professions. Anonymous illustrations, also writings of Desi Arnaz, Thomas E. Dewey, Henry Fonda.*

*14. Making Your Mark . . . 141*
*Your signature's way of revealing the essence of your individual personality, your desire to assert yourself and your sense of importance. Illustrations: including Prime Minister Mac-Millan, President F. D. Roosevelt, Fidel Castro, Nikita Khrushchev, Ben-Gurian, Noel Coward, Kaiser Wilhelm.*

*Charts . . . . . . . . . 153*
*The Pressure of Your Pen, The Significance of Various Loop Formations.*

*Introduction*

Your pen is vibrant with your thoughts and feelings as you write. Graphology is not fortune-telling but the scientific study of personality and character, revealed in the recorded motion of handwriting.

For centuries, various intellectuals throughout the world realized that human nature is revealed through motion and that in handwriting the motion is captured.

"Handwriting is a portrait of the mind," stated an Oriental philosopher many hundreds of years ago.

In 1632, an Italian named Camillo Baldo wrote a small book with a long name, *"Tratto come una lettra missive si cognoscano la natura del scrittore"* (how to know the nature and qualities of a person by looking at a letter he has written).

Two centuries later, Abbé Flandrin, a brilliant French monk, decided to determine whether or not handwriting actually does reveal character and how traits are disclosed.

Abbé Flandrin took nothing for granted in his research, and the study of handwriting became his life's work. He compared, sorted, systematized, and investigated thousands of writings.

A disciple of his, Abbé Jean-Hippolyte Michon, was both gifted and meticulous. In 1872, after thirty years of painstaking research, Abbé Michon published his findings. He titled his book, *"Les mystères de l'écriture,"* and referred to the new study as *"Graphologie."* In 1878, he published another book, *"La méthode pratique de graphologie."* The books created a stir, attracting public interest and many scholars.

J. Crepieux-Jamin, a successor of Michon, laid the cornerstone for modern graphology. He stressed that handwriting must be considered as a whole, not only according to each letter form or the t-bars, i-dots, and flourishes.

The absence of a given sign, he discovered, did not necessarily mean the trait was lacking, nor did one sign cancel the significance of another. Human nature is complex, sometimes even contradictory.

Crepieux-Jamin worked with Alfred Benet, the founder of intelligence tests, and Benet helped him to establish that honesty and intelligence are indicated in handwriting.

About the turn of the century, German scientists became interested in graphology. They based their original study upon the French findings, but soon formulated a new approach and claimed to be the leaders.

Swiss graphologists became the most highly regarded in the twenties under the leadership of Max Pulver, who demonstrated the manner in which conscious and unconscious drives are projected into handwriting. Graphology is held in very high regard in Switzerland, with courses offered in most of the colleges and universities.

The late Dr. Louise Rice introduced graphology to this country as a practical tool. She wrote several books, taught a useful system of analysis, and founded the American Graphological Society.

Scotland Yard employs graphologists. So does our own FBI. While in Switzerland, I was informed that nine out of ten Swiss business houses engage licensed staff graphologists to screen personnel.

A certain company specializing in aptitude tests sent a sales representative to Germany a few years ago. The salesman told me on his return from Germany: "I couldn't do a thing. Everywhere I went they told me the same thing, 'We use handwriting,'—frankly, I thought they were crazy! When I returned to this country, I saw your column in a New York newspaper and wrote to you for an analysis of my own writing. There was everything in that analysis that had shown up when I was given my company's test—and more!"

Americans are sometimes startled by the trust in the judgment of graphologists that they find abroad. One woman told me that she went to a bank in Sweden and explained that she had lost her letter of credit. She was asked how much money she needed and replied, "Two thousand dollars." The bank official asked her to complete the necessary forms, which he showed to an associate. He promptly returned with the amount she had mentioned. She asked, "How can you give me all this money without checking me? You never saw me before." He replied, "Our graphologist says you are as honest as the day is long!"

Graphology is not only for the businessman. A happier home can result from better understanding. You may discover that your mate's puzzling actions are affected by supersensitivity, nervousness, self-consciousness, or some other inner problem, OR your own handwriting may give you an enlightening self-estimate.

Rev. Charles Hugo Doyle, resident chaplain and an instructor at Ladycliff College for Women, has written a book entitled, *Blame Yourself If You Pick the Wrong*

## 14  *You and Your Handwriting*

*Mate* (Nugent Press). In this book, he recommends graphology as one of the reliable ways to help in the selection of a suitable marriage partner. He also deplores that so few qualified persons in America are engaged in this profession, and says that in many cases uninformed persons pretend to be graphologists. To quote:

> Medical quacks are from time to time discovered and exposed. Their existence in no way affects the importance of medical science. There are scores of "handwriting analysts" in nightclubs and county fairs who are no more worthy of credibility than is the diagnosis of medical quacks. It is such persons who have given graphology its black eye, but in Europe, especially, graphology has been, and is now, successfully used by institutions and private persons to investigate character.

After mentioning the practical uses of graphology in business, Father Doyle continues:

> Since personality and the individuality of the writer and handwriting are inseparable then it seems only logical that graphology be used to infer character strengths and weaknesses in the interest of happy and holy wedlock.

Heartache, even heartbreak, may be averted by better understanding between husband and wife. A shocking episode impressed this upon me. A man brought me the handwriting of his wife for analysis. The note was written in a foreign language so that the words were unintelligible to me. The indications of illness and depression, however, were unmistakable in the faltering strokes and sinking lines of writing.

"Be very gentle with her," I told him. "She is at a low ebb, mentally and physically, and cannot restore herself without help. Surround her with kind, encouraging associates. Never say an unkind word to her."

To my horror he suddenly burst into tears. The page of writing he had handed me was his wife's suicide note! He had come too late.

# you and your handwriting

# one
## *Your Self-Image*

Meet yourself.

Your handwriting as a whole expresses your full personality, but there is one particular letter that is an especially intimate expression of your ego. As you write capital *I*, you draw your own self-image.

You may be surprised to discover what you really think of yourself—like the seventeen-year-old girl who remarked, "I know I'm not conceited because I'm sure I know much more than I think I do."

Capital *I* is measured in relation to the writer's small or "minimum" letters. A simply-formed, moderate-sized *I* approximately two and one-half times the size of the small or minimum letters indicates confidence without vanity, as in the handwriting of FBI Director J. Edgar Hoover.

*(See next page)*

*Dear Miss Stafford:*
*I am interested in the science*

*J. Edgar Hoover*

An unobtrusive *I* in a highly simplified handwriting, as in President Kennedy's Inaugural Speech (see Chapter 21 for sample) indicates sublimation of self at the time of writing.

Distortion of *I* can indicate distortion of the self-image. For instance, Boris Karloff, star of so many horror movies, writes an *I* that appears to have two heads.

*I hope you can read this but I doubt it*

*Boris Karloff*

The small, twisted *I* in this handwriting indicates a distortion of the writer's self-image due to self-consciousness.

*I was thinking of you standing*

Writers who tend to simplify or print *I* are creatively gifted. A gracefully curved and unique *I* indicates originality, also a gracious personality. Over-ornamented *I* indicates vanity, sometimes vulgarity.

The note written by playwright Thornton Wilder illustrates the ultra-simplified, straight-line *I* in a highly creative handwriting.

*Dear Miss Stafford, here I am exposed and helpless — Temper justice with mercy! Cordially yours, Thornton Wilder*

You may emphasize self-importance in your *I* in some unusual way. A subtle elevation of the ego is shown here. Although *I* is not exaggerated in height, every *I* is un-

*When I graduated I*

derlined in a way that puts it on a little pedestal. The writer demands much of life and love, and, in fact, spent four pages to tell me so. Every sentence in her letter contained at least one *I*, similarly pedestaled.

When your *I* is high and wide, you enjoy the limelight and love attention. You dramatize yourself and may seek the stage or some position where you can be the whole show.

A large left-slanted *I* seems to contradict itself. The writer desires to be important but feels unappreciated, may fear to assert himself.

*I couldn't resist*

When *I* is so narrow that the downstroke retraces the upstroke, the writer is self-conscious, sometimes timid. This *I* is traced and also left-slanted. Timid self-efface-

*It pleases me. I*

ment is shown. Lack of self-assurance and fear of others hold back the writer and make him unable to assert himself effectively.

An odd self-effacement is illustrated here. Although his *I* is forcefully written and of impressive size, the writ-

er slants letters leftward, and he carefully crosses out his *I* with a heavy downstroke. He also crosses out the first initial of his given name. I said to him, "A strong personality is shown in your handwriting, also the desire to dominate, but you seem to fight this feeling as if you felt it wrong. This is likely to have begun as a child. Was your father over-strict?" The writer agreed emphatically. He resembles his father, yet, having been made to feel as a child that he must appear submissive, he still subconsciously negates the force of his personality by slanting letters leftward and crossing out letters that refer to himself, such as *I* and *J*, the first initial of his given name.

Teenagers (especially boys, I have noted) frequently reveal a sense of inadequacy in the formation of *I*. This is the handwriting of a seventeen-year-old boy who

*I've often considered studying*

states: "My problem is that people don't seem to want to associate with me. I don't think they dislike me but they think I am boring company." His *I* hit a real low as he wrote, "I've often considered studying psychology but feel that with my social problems I wouldn't be an appropriate person." Good intelligence and a keen, analytical mind are apparent in his writing, but letters are shaken by the writer's feeling of insecurity. His personality may improve as he matures, especially if he is encouraged by his teachers and parents. He needs to have his "self-image" built up.

A teenager's opinion of himself may be difficult to determine from the way he acts. In fact, he may pretend to be self-important to cover an inner sense of inadequacy. The size and shape of his *I* can help you to know whether he is acting as he does because of too much ego, or because of an inner sense of insecurity that he doesn't want to have discovered.

The boy who wrote these words is another teenager. His tall upper loops indicate high ideals, but his con-

*I'll attend*

trasting low *I* reflects a feeling of insignificance. His girl considers him inconsiderate because he never phones her. She does not realize that his self-appraisal is below par and that he is shy and sensitive. He tries to hide his true self-estimate by pretending indifference.

A rounded *I*, when incurved at the base, indicates a self-protective ego. Here this self-protective feeling is combined with dramatization of self according to the height and extreme width of the *I*.

*I don't know*

The *I* here is also rounded but of modest height, simply formed, right-slanted, with neat, rounded minimum

*I have an opportunity*

letters. This writer is a devoted mother whose protective instincts center around her children.

Elaboration of *I*, as here, shows conceit. This young lady has been married three times—"all failures." She must subconsciously realize that she causes her marriage failures, because in her letter she wrote, "Perhaps I can not or will not see what is the matter."

*You and Your Handwriting*

*Perhaps I can not*

One who feels unimportant and disapproved of can be more difficult than an egotist.

Your *I* may show that your self-estimate varies. In this handwriting (a confirmed bachelor) there are three *I*'s, all of different heights. The size of *I* is apparently affected by the thought that accompanies it. "I am interested" starts with a capital of moderate height, but the *I* sinks down to the height of minimum letters in "I

*I am interested, I must confess
Once I am a bachelor.*

must confess," as if the writer psychologically humbled himself at the thought of "confessing." The third *I* is three or four times as high as the minimum letters as he writes with pride, "I am a bachelor."

An angular, pointed *I* denotes a person who feels on the defensive and/or self-conscious regarding himself. His disposition may be prickly. These two specimens also show angular letters *I*.

*I am 26 years old*

*I have been dating*

Those who write with unique *I*'s as illustrated here, strive to be different. This writer crosses out the down-

*I be apt to marry*

stroke that could signify *I* with a wavy, graceful gesture of the pen. She is insecure as regards herself.

My observation has been that a devoted mother and homemaker frequently sublimates her own ego in her absorption with those for whom she cares, writing a capital *I* that is low and protectively rounded.

It is interesting to watch the evolution of a child's ego over the years, as his *I* develops and changes in size, shape, and general appearance. You will be better able to know how to help him to know himself when you are aware of the changes of self-regard being reflected in his handwriting.

## Comparison of the Self-Image in Marriage

When trouble occurs in a marriage, a comparison of *I* as written by husband and wife can be enlightening. In the sample of this married couple, SHE writes with a large emphasized *I*; HE forms a slanted, exceptionally low-topped *I* that seems almost to lie on the line. The wife wrote to complain that her husband "spoils the children," is "jealous and always picking on me."

*I am thinking of* — He

*I have married* — She

A comparison of their capitals *I* indicates that the wife takes over authority and assumes family leadership. This may have contributed towards her husband's feeling of insignificance as revealed in his *I*. His writing also reveals that he is extremely emotional and lacking in emotional control. His letters are hurriedly and unevenly written with angular tops, slanting far to the right.

His wife's handwriting denotes a self-controlled, precise temperament. Her letters are carefully formed, evenly spaced, the letter *r* made with the careful top that indicates a perfectionist. She is puzzled by the way her husband acts because his qualities are so opposed to her own. Awareness of his frustrations and problems, as revealed in his low, over-slanted *I* and his nervous, almost frantic, pen motion can help her to improve her domestic situation. She might take care to build him up rather than chide him, especially in the presence of the children. He wouldn't be so likely to think later that he must justify himself to them by "spoiling" them.

There is a further consideration here. Letter *g* is heavy but unlooped in the man's writing—in fact, he finishes no loops in the lower zone, indicating an unsatisfied sex nature. This could be a reason for his uncooperative actions.

Any woman whose *I* shows too much emphasis upon her self-image, as in this handwriting, can defeat her marriage by trying to be both mother and father. Also, without realizing it, she may humiliate her husband in their personal life.

Everything in a writing should be comparatively considered. You may feel (or wish to feel) superior to someone you refer to in your page of writing. If so, your *I* may rear up.

This writer says in her letter, "My mother is dead set against the fellow I'm to marry. She says my marrying him will be a serious mistake." The *I* is tall and self-assured in this writing. The *S* in "She" referring to her

*I am to marry She says*

mother is much lower. The writer either feels (or wishes to feel) that she knows more than her mother does.

Conversely, you may have a sense of inferiority regarding a person if you write *I* much lower than the initial letter of his name.

To "know thyself" is wisdom. You have begun in handwriting with the consideration of you, as you truly see yourself. Now comes what you ARE.

# two
## *You as an Entity*

A handwriting, like a human body, is made up of many parts, each related to the other. Glance over a page of writing as you would appraise a new acquaintance from his or her appearance. Is the general effect pleasing? Are capitals and small letters in good proportion? What is emphasized? What is unusual?

Does the writing instrument move smoothly across the page—or instead, does the writer seem driven by intensity of thought or emotion? Are strokes strong or weak, graceful or awkward, gentle or sharp? Are letters original or conventional? Do they appear cramped, or are they generously widespread? Does the pen appear to plod slowly across the page—or to fly so swiftly that many letters are indistinguishable?

Your handwriting as a whole expresses your personality so succinctly that even your personal tastes may be gauged. A leading Fifth Avenue department store once engaged my services to select a suitable handwriting for each of several styles of stationery to be used in a newspaper advertisement. They showed me various letterheads: highly stylized, "cute," impressive, unobtrusive, gay, precise, artistic, fastidious, warmly colorful—and I selected a handwriting to appear on each. When I had made my selections, the store manager surprised me. One by one, he called in the girls whose writing I had chosen and asked each to select the letterhead she preferred. In every case the girl chose the letterhead assigned for her handwriting, although one girl did choose two letterheads.

*Development of Individuality*

You may have noticed that the appearance of your writing has changed over the years. As you mature, your handwriting expresses your development.

When a baby is born it looks very much like all other babies, but soon begins to have an appearance and personality of its own. Thus it is with handwriting. A child learning to write strives to conform to model letters. He is more absorbed in the formation of letters than in the thought being expressed. As he gains confidence he writes with increasing spontaneity and his individuality begins to show in deviations from the copybook model letters.

Individuality in handwriting may begin to show early, as I discovered when teaching first grade. In fact, this discovery set me on the road to becoming a graphologist, because I had just been reading Dr. Louise Rice's book *Personality in Handwriting*. Was it true that we disclose ourselves as we write? I was interested but dubious.

Then, one day after my pupils had left, I saw a practice writing sheet lying on the schoolroom floor. Glancing at it, I thought, "Arthur has forgotten to put his name on his paper." Suddenly I had a realization that changed the whole course of my life. All thirty of my first-graders had been taught to write similarly, yet somehow Arthur had given his writing the stamp of his individuality so that I was able to pick it out from the others. From then on, I studied graphology rather than reading about it casually. A new world opened to me—I felt as if I had begun really to see and understand people.

## Simplification versus Elaboration

The purpose of handwriting is to convey thought. You cannot write faster than you think. A pen gains speed by simplifying the pen motion. Simplification is an indication of maturity, alertness, intelligence, and spontaneity.

Persons engaged in self-assertive effort or creative ideas are less inclined to make conventional letter forms than those whose work requires regimentation of thought and effort. An organization with the stated purpose of stemming the "increasing illegibility" of handwriting discovered that the officials in a business house were much more likely to write "illegibly" than were the stenographers or accountants.

Swiftness of thought can speed pen motion to such an extent that the handwriting appears illegible. When this is accompanied by extreme simplification, a brilliant, creative mind is indicated.

President J. F. Kennedy's handwriting as he com-

*President John Kennedy's Inaugural address*

posed his Inaugural Speech reflects a high pitch of creative thought. His pen sped swiftly across the page, with ultra-simplification of letters. He discarded beginning and ending strokes of words; frequently strokes between letters were also discarded.

As his ideas were correlated, words were frequently crossed out and others substituted. His forceful horizontal strokes show a strong will. Sometimes horizontal strokes (including t-bars) end sharply and aggressively in his writing—and at other times with a tiny hook, indicating perseverance and persistence. ("Hooks cling" is a popular saying among graphologists.) Certain letters stand out with clarity and significance. The 8-shaped *g* in the word "beginning" and the two-stroke capital *T* emphasize cultured tastes as well as high intelligence.

Simplification does not, necessarily, cause a writing to be illegible. Morton Yarman, an editor of "Parade"

*Dear Muriel,*

*Here is a sample of my handwriting. Hope it's what you can use.*

*Morton Yarman*

*You as an Entity* 35

and the author of many factual books, writes with letters that are highly simplified, yet clearly legible.

Deliberate illegibility is shown in the handwriting of Celia Sanchez. Her upper loops are inflated in a way that crosses out everything she's written. She was Fidel Castro's close accomplice, companion, and advisor during and after the Cuban revolution. Elaboration of strokes for the purpose of accenting illegibility indicates secrecy and deceit.

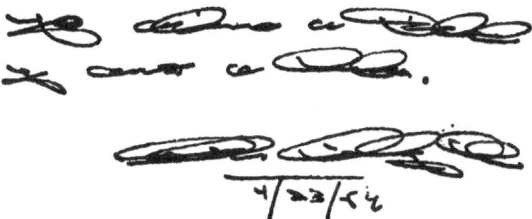

*Celia Sanchez*

There is another type of elaboration that attempts to dramatize the writer. Large letters and many flourishes, as in the writing of Jayne Mansfield, are obviously attention compelling.

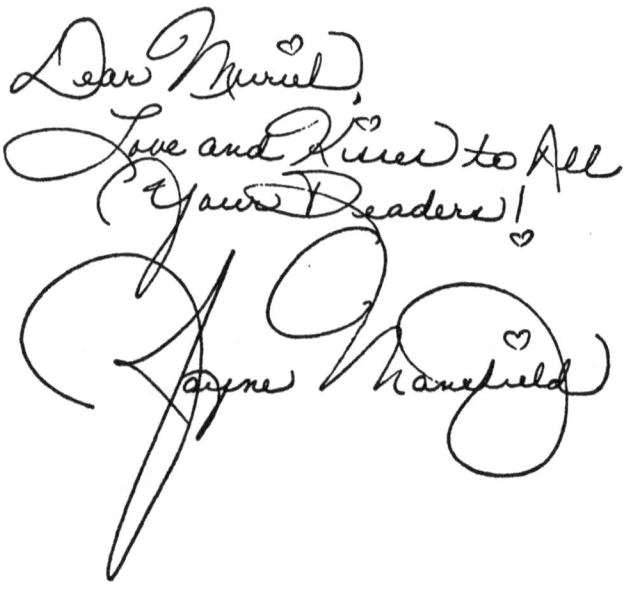

*Simplification and Elaboration*

You may soon find yourself attracted to a person, or otherwise, according to the appearance of his handwriting—but do not make snap judgments. Analyze every handwriting thoroughly before coming to a full conclusion.

The importance of using tested rules and criteria was pointed out to me early in my career by no less an authority than Dr. Alfred Adler. The noted Viennese psychiatrist was traveling in this country *incognito* a few months before his death in 1937. I was invited by his secretary to meet him, because of my column on graphology in a Chicago newspaper. In the course of our conversation, Dr. Adler expressed great interest and knowledge of graphology. He told me that at the time, he was doing "an extensive study of the significance of i-dots." Replying to my request for a sample of his writing, he wrote as follows: "Handwriting is frozen movement. When interpreting movement, especially frozen movement, be careful. Never use your own individual interpretation."

> Dear Miss Stafford
> handwriting is frozen movement.
> To interpret movement, especially frozen movement
> be careful. Do not give interpretations in your
> own individual conception.
>                                    Alfred Adler

*Dr. Alfred Adler*


Human nature is so complicated and variable that opposing traits may sometimes be discovered in the same writing.

Whether a trait is "good" or "bad" depends largely upon how the trait is used. For instance, one who is high-principled can be an inspiration to others—or be too self-righteous. Modesty is a virtue—but lack of self-appreciation can cause you to hide your light beneath a bushel.

Some people live and die with potentialities that are never realized. If Grandma Moses had died at sixty-nine she would never have found that she had the talent to become a famous artist. It is interesting to speculate how much a talent would have been indicated by her handwriting prior to this discovery.

# three
*Invisible Borders*

*Margins*

You may build a border or fence around your house for privacy, to protect your property, or because you are afraid. So it is with margins.

The margins that surround a page of your handwriting are invisible borders within which, through the motion of your pen, you express your innermost thoughts, feelings, ambitions. Margins are placed with subconscious exactness. Motion pictures taken of persons while writing disclose that a writer pauses a fraction of a second at the beginning of each line.

On the left side of the page, the depth of the margin is an indication of the distance that you put between yourself and others, also between yourself and what is past.

An extremely deep margin on the left side of the page but not on the right side, indicates subconscious desire to escape from past experiences or remembrances. This may begin to show in one's handwriting after a tragically unhappy experience. When Debbie Reynolds wrote for my analysis as a starlet, her note was placed in the center of the page. Some time later, after the conclusion of her disastrous marriage to Eddie Fisher, she wrote another note for my newspaper column. This time, her left-side margin was so deep that the note seemed to begin in the center of the page, with no margin on the right.

The left and right margins have opposing connotations. As an exaggerated left margin reveals a desire to

*This is my handwriting*
*All my Best wishes*
*Debbie*
*Reynolds*

> I think your analyzing my hand writing was terrific
>
> Love
> Debbie
> Reynolds

forget the past, an exaggerated right margin reveals anxiety regarding what is ahead. A feeling of apprehension may cause you to write with a deeper-than-usual right margin.

Since a wide margin on the left is an invisible wall of discretion, any decreasing of width towards the bottom of the page indicates a lowering of the guard.

Widening of left margin shows an increasing sense of caution. The writer may promise more at first than he cares to fulfill later.

A widening of right margin indicates increasing shyness, fear, or suspicion. If the right margin narrows, guardedness is being replaced by increasing interest and confidence.

No margins at all, so that each line of writing begins at the left edge of the paper and continues all the way to the right, denotes that the bars are down—the writer is interested to know you and all about you. He is neighborly, loquacious, eager to be of help. He may also be curious and have a tendency to gossip.

Margins frequently vary according to the writer's feeling of cordiality towards the one to whom he is writing. Wide margins are formal, narrow margins informal.

When your right margin is extremely irregular, you have an inconsistent temperament, and find it hard to settle down. You may be penny-wise and pound-foolish. Travel and adventure appeal to you. You are sometimes outgoing and at other times guarded, even antagonistic, towards the very people you love most.

A deep margin, equidistant on all four sides, reveals a reserved and aesthetic nature. Creative artistic talent evidenced in a writing is accented by a framelike margin.

Margins filled with scribblings denote a frugal nature —when the writing is highly simplified, a lively mind striving to catch and preserve rapid-occurring thoughts and ideas.

The significance of upper and lower margins is more difficult to establish. Generally, deep upper margin indicates formality of approach. No upper margin indicates informality, sometimes abruptness; also, in some cases, frugality.

The lower margin may be narrow because the writer is carried away with his ideas, thoughts, and philosophies—or his loquaciousness—and neglects to stop writing until the paper gives out.

## *Spacing*

Besides margins, there are other significant spacings in a handwriting, including the space between letters, be-

*Invisible Borders* 43

tween words, and between lines of writing. A well-balanced handwriting is likely to have well-balanced spacing. Any pronounced widening or narrowing of spaces is significant.

Letters that appear extremely tall in proportion to the space between letters indicate restriction of thought. The writer is likely to be set in his opinions and difficult to dissuade.

*had my writing analyzed*

Wide spaces between letters indicate generosity. Carried to an extreme, however, over-wide spaces may indicate a shallow mind.

*I am forty-seven,*

In cursive writing we are taught to connect letters in a single word. Writers who continue to do so are matter-of-fact, conventional, logical, reasonable, realistic, and may be somewhat unimaginative.

*I am 17 and will be a
senior this fall. I hope*

The omission of connective strokes between letters of a word is a form of simplification. The disconnection of letters is an indication of an inventive, independent mind, artistic, intuitive thinking and acting. This can be carried to an extreme. When almost all letters are unconnected, the writer is discursive, restless, egocentric, may not finish everything he starts to do. If the first letter of a word frequently stands apart and the other letters are connected, the writer is cautious and may have a tendency to procrastinate.

*The weather spell takes*

*To who it may*

*Invisible Borders* 45

When all letters are connected except the last letter of a word, the writer vacillates and postpones. When everything seems settled, he suddenly has another thought. He puts off coming to definite conclusions.

The small letter *i* may stand in the middle of a word, disconnected from the other letters. (Even the small letter *i* is sometimes an expression of the ego. When *i* stands alone, the writer is individualistic, independent.)

*give an analysis*

*Space Between Words*

Small, even spaces between words in good proportion to the size of the letters are indications of good balance. A homemaker with a strong sense of order is likely to write with small even spaces between letters; so is an accountant or a specialist concentrating upon details. Over-wide spaces between words may emphasize introversion or loneliness. Those who place words like little islands in a wide sea of space are often interested in poetry, music, or literature. They have deep-rooted feelings and convictions.

Uneven spaces between words should be considered according to the development of the handwriting. Confusion of thought, hesitation, and low mentality are emphasized if the letters are undeveloped and the spaces between words uneven. In a simplified handwriting that indicates high intelligence, the writer is unpredictable, somewhat inconsistent.

## Space Between Lines

Lines of writing that stand clearly apart show a good organizer who strives towards logical and reasonable presentation. The ability to concentrate clearly is indicated.

*Dear Miss Clifford —*

*I'm glad you think*

*I'm conscientious —*

*Adlai S. Stevenson*

Spaces between lines can be over-wide. If so, the writer is trying too hard to be logical, conscientious, and coherent. This can be due to fear of making a mistake.

The more narrow the space between lines, the less reserve the writer is likely to have. When lines run into each other so that they overlap, confusion of thought is indicated.

oposit sex and do, am
trying to find a life mate
clubs that advertize in cert.

# four
## *So Leans Your Heart*

As your letters lean, so leans your heart. You bend towards others sympathetically when warmly inclined. If not, you assume a stiffer, withdrawn attitude. Your handwriting does the same.

A right slant of letters is a "towards" or outgoing motion because the pen moves rightward across the page. The more the downstrokes of your writing lean towards the right, the more you are directly impelled by your feelings, sympathies, and desires.

You can change the slant of your letters from your own true slant for only as long as the conscious effort lasts. The second that you stop concentrating upon this change your handwriting will slip into the slant that expresses your true emotional leanings. A writing sample with a deliberately artificial slant of letters is useless for purposes of analysis.

The direction of letter slant changes over the years, according to the writer's change of heart or emotional development. At age twelve Elizabeth Taylor leaned letters only slightly rightward. By the time she had reached eighteen, her letters leaned much more rightward.

*Dear Miss Stafford*
*I think this is a wonderful*
*Elizabeth Taylor*

*Age 12*

*Dear Miss Stafford*
*I can not*
*think of anything*
*very clever to*
*say —*
*Elizabeth*
*Taylor*

*Age 18*

*You and Your Handwriting*

A moderately rightward slant of letters indicates a warmhearted, affectionate nature ("love interest"). Unless letters are wide, the writer may not be able to express his feelings and is over-sensitive.

*love interest*

Letters that slant too far towards the right reveal a lack of emotional control ("don't leave me").

*don't leave*

Left-slant of letters is usually rooted in childhood experiences that have caused the writer to feel rejected, lonely, and/or insecure. This is the handwriting of a bachelor, in his thirties, whose mother was an invalid throughout his childhood from the age of seven.

*The rumor has it that*

*So Leans Your Heart* 51

Your favorite singer may or may not be as romantic as he sounds. Perry Como's handwriting, slanted vigorously rightward, indicates a deeply emotional nature.

Another popular singer wrote the sample "I can really create." His letter-slant indicates that he is introverted, more interested in creative accomplishment than in romance.

You lead with your heart if strokes of writing slant far rightward from the very first word. Letters sloping farther and farther rightward as a page of writing progresses indicates increasing interest and warmth of feeling.

A decrease of slant or sudden change to left slant in a page of writing indicates that skepticism is stronger than confidence. In these lines of writing by Premier Nehru, the body of the note slants rightward and the signature leftward. He is sincere and well-meaning, but disillusionment has made him wary.

*All good wishes for the season and the New Year.*

*Jawaharlal Nehru*

*Premier Nehru*

When a signature is *more* right-slanted than the body of the writing, a certain hypocrisy is evident. The writer is inwardly more skeptical or withdrawn than he wishes you to know.

Your handwriting is as consistent as you are. Some people write with right-slanted letters when they feel warmly inclined, but at other times slant letters towards the left, implying a change of heart.

Vertical letters denote an independent nature, not much affected by the emotions of others. This may show the writer to be aloof but compelling, or in a light-pressured writing to be merely unresponsive.

If you write with letters that slant very little or not at

all, you are independent. You do as you wish. The world is your stage, and when you wish you can put on a fitting mask. You distrust emotionalism.

Men who write with vertical or very slightly slanted letters are frequently bachelors. Sometimes caution is emphasized because of the writer's particular vocation, as in the handwriting of J. Edgar Hoover. His small letters lean very slightly back from the center. Interestingly, he has never married.

The appearance of a writer and the publicity given to him can be misleading. Husky actor Richard Burton is headlined as an extreme romanticist, but he writes with short vertical strokes. At the time I analyzed his handwriting, he remarked, "Yes, it's true that I am an introvert. The trouble is, nobody believes me." A combination of emotional suppression and creative talent is apparent in this sample.

*Dear Muriel,*
*I shall be absolutely fascinated.*
*Richard Burton*

A man who delays marriage indefinitely and blames the other party may have a mother fixation if letters do not slant rightward. The young man who wrote the following note (on his mother's stationery) uses small vertical letters with left-slanted t-bars. "My ex-fiancée fell madly in love with another man and broke off our romance of twelve years. I presume the infatuation will wear off and then comes the question of whether I should marry her."

*He*

*She*

This indignant young man did not explain why his romance had stretched into twelve years. He merely felt abused that his longtime fiancée should consider another man. Her softly rounded letters, leaning moderately rightward, indicate that she is certainly not one to fall impulsively in love. She is affectionate, considerate, tolerant.

More women than men write with vertical or left-slanted letters. Girls are more often separated from their fathers as children than boys are from their mothers. In the normal circumstances of domestic life, the mother

*So Leans Your Heart* 55

usually spends more time in the home than does the father. According to Freudian theory, her father is a girl's first love, and a boy's first love is his mother. At the time of a divorce, the mother most often receives custody of the children. As a result, the boy "keeps his first love," but the girl may feel a sense of rejection that affects her all her life—and frequently shows in the direction of her letter-slant as an adult. She may compensate her desire for affection by demonstrative behavior. This may reveal itself in the effort to achieve a feeling of acceptance. She may marry more than once, or she may seek a career that will give her the attention she yearned for as a child.

Faye Emerson was at the height of her acting career when she wrote for analysis. She was also married to El-

*Tell me my secrets —*

*Faye Emerson*

liot Roosevelt, son of the then President of the United States. Although she had great beauty and had achieved popularity, prestige, and wealth to an unusual degree, her letters leaned leftward. "Did you have a lonely or unhappy childhood?" I asked. Faye nodded and replied, "My parents died when I was two years old and I was brought up by a succession of foster-parents. I always felt unwanted."

"Your sense of rejection could hurt your marriage," I said, "you may never feel that your husband really loves you." "That's exactly what happened," she replied. I did not know that she had been through one divorce and had begun proceedings against Elliot Roosevelt.

A man whose letters slant leftward may have the same compulsion to achieve popular approval, because of separation from his mother (or worry concerning her) as a child. Victor Borge was a child genius. He told me, "I was a concert pianist from the age of eight and had to travel continuously from city to city. I missed my mother. She was a wonderful person. I used to think of her when I was away and how I would throw my arms about her when I saw her and tell her how much I loved her. But when she opened the door, all I could say was 'Hi.'" As an adult, Victor has practically discarded the concert work to become a pianist-comedian.

In marriage, overemotionalism in one partner and unresponsiveness in the other can lead to disaster. A man who was receiving psychological treatment without results wrote with letters that slanted extremely rightward. I was consulted about his handwriting, and requested a sample of his wife's writing. I was told, "She is a perfect angel. I don't know how anybody else could put up with him." Yet her handwriting revealed a cold, unresponsive nature. Blaming himself for her lack of emo-

> Dear Muriel,
> The study of handwriting is most interesting, and I hope that, some day, you will tell me more about it.
> Sincerely,
> Cordell Hull

tional response, her overemotional husband had not mentioned his problem to the psychiatrist. The wife was examined by a doctor and discovered to be frigid. The husband's ego was thus relieved from the feeling of guilt when he realized that his wife was unable to respond emotionally.

Letters slanting in various directions within the same line of writing, sometimes within the same word, denote emotional conflict or indecision. A temporary conflict of letter slant may occur following disturbing news. In the note below written by Secretary of State Cordell Hull, a conflict of letter slant is pronounced.

## 58  *You and Your Handwriting*

The day that he wrote this note Secretary Hull had just received word that the Germans were marching through Holland, and he knew that war was imminent.

You may find yourself writing with letters that conflict in slant during a period of emotional uncertainty.

There are other causes for unsteady letter slant. An adult handwriting that habitually wavers back and forth in slant may indicate a tendency to play both ends against the middle, or to try to please too many people at the same time.

*Miss Murice Stafford —*
*Speciman of my handwriting —*
*Cordeel Hull*

An immature handwriting with an uncertain letter slant may show uncertainty of self. The writer is striving towards identity.

*I am 16 years old*

*So Leans Your Heart* 59

A tense writing in which the letter slant is disturbed may indicate a writer who needs medical attention and much consideration. The writer of "doing the best I can" was recovering from a nervous breakdown. His wife complained that he did not work and blamed his parents for having "babied him." He needed sympathy and encouragement rather than criticism.

*doing the best I can*

If your mate or a friend slants letters far to the left, do not be misled by his possibly gay manner. He tends to feel misunderstood and may cover cynicism with irony or wit—if the handwriting is simplified.

*to tell you how*

# five
## *Emotional Impact*

Your force of will and self-assertion are expressed in the pressure that you exert upon your pen as you write. To press deeply into the paper gives the writer a sense of overcoming obstacles and of conquering.

The strength of pen pressure is usually indicated by the darkness and width of strokes, but when there is any doubt, run your finger under the page beneath the writing. Little ridges can be felt if the pressure is excessive.

You may say that some pens write more heavily than others. This is true and can make your choice of pen significant. Greer Garson would not write for analysis until she could use her own stub pen, so she had to send her specimen from Hollywood to New York. The deliberate force of her personality is apparent in her carefully formed, thick-stroked letters.

Strong, vigorous pen pressure, especially with swift pen motion, indicates vitality and a magnetic personality. The writer's vocation should give him a chance to

*Emotional Impact* 61

show what he can do in a practical remunerative way, especially when powers of leadership are otherwise indicated throughout his writing.

One who combines force of pen pressure with indications of a charming personality may get his own way so pleasantly that he seems to be conceding rather than dominating. These fortunate persons often rise to prominence without apparent effort.

When a writing shows deep pressure with graceful, right-slanted letters, a warmth and force of personality is revealed that has sometimes changed the course of history. Never underestimate such a writer.

> Dear Miss Stafford —
> Your study of handwriting must have fascinating possibilities — What, for instance, do you make of this?
> Regards — Peer Garson.

An excellent illustration is the handwriting of the
Duchess of Windsor. Her pen moves fluidly across the

> Dear Miss Stafford
> Hand Writing
> analysis must be a
> fascinating profession
> I shall be interested in your
> reading of mine
>
> Yours Sincerely
> Wallis Windsor

*Duchess of Windsor*

*Emotional Impact* 63

page, strokes are wide, graceful, heavy. Horizontal lines are darker on the right, showing a deepening of pressure in the t-bars and word endings. A darkening of pen pressure in horizontal strokes stresses persistence and determination.

You may mask the strength of your will and influence. If your letters are heavy-pressured and unslanted, you have a forceful, controlled will. "I look forward to seeing" reveals a powerful personality and a gifted mind.

*P.S. I look forward to seeing an outline!*

This writer's low, printed capital *I* shows that she does not allow any desire for acclaim to affect her. She is modest as well as creative. Her small letters are simplified, swiftly written, often unique, but they never lean indiscreetly leftward. She can get her way and make others think they are getting theirs. The combination of will, creative talent, and self-restraint shown in her handwriting has helped to make this writer a top career woman in the editorial field.

A compelling personality combined with showmanship is denoted by the large heavy-pressured vertical letters of Bill Cullen's writing.

*(See next page)*

*Love,*
*Bill Cullen*

If your handwriting shows unusually wide, heavy strokes, you may or may not realize how strongly you affect others, especially if letters slant leftward. Your outward appearance or manner may even seem quite the opposite from your true nature. Disguised force of will can sometimes disrupt a marriage, for the reason that no one suspects the writer is causing his or her own trouble by ruling the home with subtle tyranny.

As she made an appointment for a consultation, a lady said to me on the phone, "I'm hoping my husband's and daughter's writing will show why they can't get along together." I told her to bring some of her own handwriting with theirs.

She was a small woman, low-voiced and quietly dressed. After handing me a letter written by her daughter and a note by her husband, she gave me the third sample of writing. "Is this your writing?" I asked in astonishment. She nodded. The other writings were written with light pressure and right slant, but this third writing was bold and emphatic, with large, unslanted letters.

"You are the reason your husband and daughter cannot get along. You stand between them," I exclaimed.

She replied in her low voice, "I know that is true. They are both receiving psychiatric treatment and I wondered why their psychiatrist doesn't question me more."

How could he suspect that this unobtrusive-appearing woman could have such a compelling effect upon his distressed patients? Only her handwriting disclosed her subtle domination. Even her husband and daughter did not realize what was really happening. She was a prisoner of self, unable to get help because nobody saw her as she actually was.

Her father had been tyrannical and so was she, but as so often happens, she thought her faults were her husband's. Many traits of which she complained in him were evident in her own writing instead of his. His light-pressured, right-slanted letters revealed a sensitive, responsive, loving nature.

She earnestly wished for her husband and daughter to be compatible. I suggested that her husband and daughter might take a vacation together. The result was very successful. Without the distraction of mother's compelling personality, the father and daughter were able to find each other.

When pen pressure is heavy, with the motion of the pen unsteady and slow, the writer may be "overcompensating." He is trying to assure others and himself of his strength, physically and/or psychologically. In "I am

*I am 80 years old.*

80 years old" heavy pen pressure is combined with slow pen progress and shaken letter forms.

A strong contrast of pen pressures between husband and wife distinctly reveals the truly dominant member of a family. If a husband and wife both write with unusually forceful pen pressure, there may be a struggle for dominance.

Heavy pressure is self-assertive, and so is the right slant of letters. Therefore, a conflict of drive is apparent when a left-slanted handwriting shows heavy pressure. The urge to dominate conflicts with the writer's dislike of becoming emotionally involved. These writers are

*I am contemplating*

*She*

*get together again*

*He*

usually much more likely to be attractive than attracted. This sample was written by a husband and wife. He digs heavily into the paper, but his letters are unslanted. He has been married three times but is still restless, dissatisfied. His wife's handwriting shows a submissive nature in her softly written, right-slanted letters. She tries hard to please him, but says it is impossible.

Shaded pen strokes, as illustrated in Gypsy Rose Lee's handwriting, are an indication of sensuality.

You are sensitive, responsive, imaginative, and inclined to be sentimental if your pen skims lightly over the paper with letters slanting rightward. Your desire is to please those you love and your reward is their approval.

A combination of gentle pen pressure and small, orderly, moderately slanted letters reveals spiritual absorption and devotion to duty. The delicately written handwriting of a nun is similar to hundreds of writings I have received from those who have renounced the world to serve God in a convent.

*(See next page)*

*Will you kindly analyze my handwriting*

You may write with light pressure and letters that slant far to the right. If so, choose your associates with care for you are responsive to the point of susceptibility. In marriage you need a practical, affectionate mate who respects your principles and is considerate of your sensitive feelings.

Agility of mind may contribute towards light pressure when simplified letters skim swiftly across the page.

All who write with light pressure are not angels, by any means. In the wrong environment, a young person who presses lightly upon a pen may be more easily led astray than a forceful writer. A chameleon quality accompanies faint or uncertain strokes. This may explain why a high percentage of delinquent children in institutions write with light pen pressure. Made to believe he is "bad" when barely able to understand, a child may live up to an unhappy self-image.

If you write with light pressure and letters slanting leftward, you are pulling down the shades of your mind and heart because you fear you will be hurt.

*Emotional Impact* 69

Slant of letters and pen pressure simultaneously considered reveal your emotional impact. In the chart on page 155 you will see how the significance of slant is affected by pressure of the pen.

# six

## *Your Disposition and Temperament*

Your basic disposition, temperament, and attitude towards others are reflected in the shape of your letters. If you wrote with only downstrokes and upstrokes, the result would be merely a succession of lines. The connective strokes from left to right give form and shape to your letters so that they appear rounded, pointed, "garlanded," or "thready." Most writings contain more than one type of connective, usually a significant combination of two or more.

A rounded, rooflike connective stroke is termed an "arcade," indicating a pleasant manner, inward reserve, and outward conformity. The more even-topped and consistent the arcades, the more these traits are emphasized.

Pointed connectives are termed "angles," indicating a critical, analytical, and assertive way of thought. If your handwriting looks sharply angular, you are independent, ready to act or to argue for your beliefs and desires. You may think it is your duty to "speak up," especially if the angles are right-slanted.

*neither temperament*

The writer of sample "neither temperament" admits that both he and his wife "lack the subtle approach" because neither temperament is "malleable," but he says they are "still going strong after 30 years of marriage."

"Garlands" reveal cordiality, an obliging nature, and usually a likable personality; and may be described as an upside down curve, as when *m* resembles *w* and *n* resembles *u.*

The "thread" is a wavy motion of the pen that substitutes an indistinguishable line for a letter or group of letters. Imaginative and creative persons frequently favor the thread. Politicians and statesmen sometimes use a thready line to replace letters at the end of a word, revealing a gift for diplomacy and for wiggling out of tight places.

To remember the four connectives and their basic significance, try this hand exercise:

Place your hand palm down, softly humped. This represents the protective, concealing arcade.

The angle is an aggressive motion—so draw your hand into a tight fist to designate its implications.

For the garland, place your hand with the palm up as if to shake hands (cordiality).

The thread is a sinuous motion, and it may be represented by wriggling your hand, palm downward.

A change from one connective to another can be significant according to placement. For instance, the late Dag Hammarskjold wrote his signature as a succession of tiny left-slanted garlands. At the end of his name, he

## 72  *You and Your Handwriting*

placed a firm arcade like a shut door. He was a cordial listener but noncommittal and reserved.

### *The Arcade*

Rounded connectives cover. They may shelter the quiet contemplation of a philosopher, the self-absorption of a teenager, the guilty thoughts of a criminal, the protective thoughts of a mother or teacher, the caution of a detective, even the artificial conformity of a social climber, and so on. Architects have a tendency to form sheltering arcades.

Neat, right-slanted arcades as in the handwriting of Sister Mary Rosa, a teacher, disclose affectionate protectiveness, orderliness, reserve, and dislike of contention.

*important subject*

*Sister M. Rosa*

When a writing is slowly formed with retouchings that do not add to the legibility, arcades may be deliberately concealing as in the round inflated loops of the handwriting of revolutionist Celia Sanchez (see Chapter 2).

## The Angle

The angular connective does not cover smoothly like the arcade, nor glide along easily like the garland. To make an angle, you must stop at every point where the direction changes, whether at the top or base of a letter. As a result, the speed of writing is checked.

Many engineers, physicists, and others whose work requires intense concentration and analytical insight write letters formed of small angles of regular height.

*I am beginning to think*

Large angular letters formed with heavy pen pressure and pronounced slant reveal physical assertiveness and the desire for independent action.

When letters become raggedly angular, emotional tension may be driving the writer more than he realizes. Unless checked, the result could be marital disagreements—or an ulcer.

If you write with very right-slanted, angular letters, you may precipitate a quarrel or argument and believe that the other person started the trouble. This was illustrated rather amusingly by two girls who were on vacation together. Glancing at their writings, I mentioned that the writer of rounded letters (Jane) had a pleasant, reserved disposition and that the other girl (Sara), who wrote with angular letters, was assertive and critical. Sara came to me afterward and said, "You were all wrong about Jane. She is very difficult. In fact, we had an argument at breakfast this morning and I don't think I can stand it any longer. I may go home."

"I am sure Jane isn't as difficult as you think," I replied. "Be very pleasant to her today. Never criticize her in any way, and see how she acts."

In the evening she came to me again and asked me if I had said anything to Jane about our conversation. When I replied that I had not even talked to Jane that day, Sara said, "I can't understand it. I did what you told me and she's angelic."

Compare your mate's or your child's writing with your own. You may discover that you are the one who is precipitating trouble.

*The Garland*

The garland connective is a soft-flowing gesture of the pen. The writer strives to be cordial, obliging, likable, to the degree that the writing is garlanded.

Chancellor Adenauer's signature is composed almost entirely of large garlands. His remarkable popularity has kept him at the head of his nation long beyond the age when most men are retired.

*Chancellor Adenauer*

*Your Disposition and Temperament* 75

A combination of deep garlands like deep bows begins the signature of Nikita Khrushchev's son-in-law, but sharp irregularity takes over towards the close, and the signature ends with a stabbing downthrust. Here the surface cordiality is hypocritical, does not last.

*M. Sholokhov (Khrushchev's son-in-law)*

Strong pen pressure adds a magnetic quality to the charm indicated by smooth-flowing garlands, as in the handwriting of the Duchess of Windsor. (Chapter 5)

The sample "I've enjoyed the people" shows a combination of smooth garlands with aggressive angles. The writer, a successful real estate salesman, covers his energetic assertiveness with a gracious personality.

*The Thread*

The "thread" motion is swift, elusive; revealing imagination and ingenuity. Thread connectives in a highly simplified writing indicate a race between the writer's swift mind and the recording of his thoughts on paper,

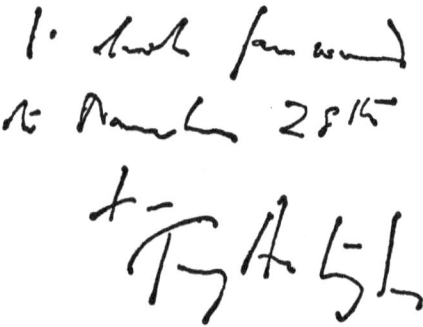

*Anthony Armstrong Jones*

as in the writing of former photographer Tony Armstrong-Jones.

Thread connectives evade formal set patterns, and the writer too is unconventional, individualistic. Class distinctions are strong in England, yet Tony Armstrong-Jones, a commoner, wooed and won the Princess Margaret.

I had the opportunity to analyze their writings for a London publication just before the wedding. My wonder was what would happen when the formality of royal living closed in around him. His first publicized action when he returned from his honeymoon was dismissal of the butler. Soon afterwards, he dismissed his "gentleman's gentleman." Instead of settling down to the formal routine of royal living, he found a creative outlet with a newspaper.

Many authors use the thread connective, and it is always an indication of a "gift for gab" whether the words are spoken or written.

Jimmy Durante's quick wit is reflected in the many smooth-flowing thread connectives throughout his writing. Only three or four letters are fully formed in his signature.

Since Jimmy pretends to be such an extrovert, the left slant of his letters was surprising, but he admitted that he does have a buried sense of rejection—because of his nose. He told me that when he was young he didn't think any girl would want to be seen with him.

> Dear Muriel —
> I can stand looking at the looking Glass
> But can this looking Glass stand looking at me —
> I loves ya
> *Jimmy*

*Jimmy Durante*

## *Connectives Between Letters*

Discarding of connectives between letters of a word has been discussed in Chapter 2. The writer who simplifies his writing in this manner is intuitive and quick-witted. He always has the right word at the right time. He acts directly upon his hunches if letters slant rightward. If letters slant leftward, he analyzes them first to know why they are good.

The disconnection of letters is a creative indication, especially when capitals are printed, as in the writing of Thornton Wilder.

All letters of a word carefully connected is an indication that the writer is logical and does not rush to conclusions.

# seven
## *Your Libido*

Your subconscious attitude towards spiritual, material, and social values is reflected in the three "zones" of your handwriting.

As you write across the page, you reach up into the upper zone and down into the lower zone to form upper and lower loops. The central zone does not reach either up or down. This is the zone of "social consciousness." Letters that have no loops are completely in the central zone. These include: a, c, e, m, n, o, r, s, u, v, w, z.

In the area of upper loops, you reveal your idealistic aspirations. In the lower zone, the area of lower loops, you reveal your attitude towards money and/or sex.

A well-balanced personality is indicated if all zones are given consideration.

Bob Hope's handwriting gives full emphasis to every zone, with the dramatic flourish of a showman.

*(See next page)*

*Dear Muriel:*
*Thanks for the*
*Memory —*
*Bob Hope*

The signature of the Reverend James Keller, originator and director of the Christophers, illustrates all three zones in a rhythmical, simplified script.

*God bless you*

*James Keller*

*Your Libido* 81

The simple *K* aspires with graceful dignity. Both upper and lower loops of *J* are wide and full, denoting a combination of spirituality (above) and awareness of material needs (below), but the lower loop is double crossed, indicating a sublimation of sex, due to the writer's vow of celibacy. The central zone has right-slanted, rounded letters, revealing a protective, warmhearted social consciousness.

Father Keller uses the creative talent evident in his writing to help others find God. The theme of the Christophers is from the words of St. Christopher: "Better to light one candle than to curse the darkness." Besides his work with the Christophers, Father Keller writes books and a syndicated newspaper column to help support his idealistic purpose. He also conducts his own television program dedicated to the purpose of carrying his message and raising funds to help him do so.

A normally completed lower loop is one that crosses the downstroke on the left. Smoothly completed lower loops, right-slanted and in good proportion to the writing as a whole, indicate emotional maturity and a satisfied libido.

Exaggerated lower loops, so big that they are out of proportion to the other zones, are nick-named "moneybags" by graphologists. Besides the ability to make money, they indicate a strong sex nature and, usually, good vitality.

## 82  *You and Your Handwriting*

Heavy pressure in the lower zone emphasizes materialistic or sexual desire. Lower loops that run into the line below denote emotional restlessness that may interfere with the writer's mental concentration.

Swelled lower loops, slanted leftward, sometimes indicate obsession with the accumulation of money due to the writer's sense of insecurity. The specimen "stingy wife" was sent to me by her husband, who bitterly complained of her "stinginess," as follows:

*a good position*

*He*

*sympathies to you*

*She*

I have a good position and give her a nice allowance but she even fights over paying a nickel for a paper. She asks the neighbors for the leftover clothes and it is very embarrassing. When we have important people for dinner (very seldom) she makes a miserable hamburg roast though I give her extra money. I hate stingy people and to live with one is disgusting. As she gets older it is worse.

*Your Libido* 83

The husband's writing is light pressured and extremely right-slanted, reflecting an impractical nature that may have intensified his wife's fear of spending.

Odd-shaped lower loops may stress immaturity and/or a neurosis. In this sample, the lower loops are flourished and incomplete. All downstrokes slant leftward

and so do the word endings (towards self). A self-absorbed libido is indicated here. Excessive pen pressure and large middle zone indicate the writer's inward desire to be outgoing, but she is a prisoner of her inhibitions.

Another immature and fearful libido is indicated in the sample that reads, "My boy friend & I." This writer apparently attempts to repress sexual thoughts (left-slanted *y*) in contradiction to the naturally affectionate nature indicated in the right-slanted upper and middle zone of her writing. If she began to slant lower loops

84  *You and Your Handwriting*

leftward during her friendship with the boy, he is probably the cause of her complex. However, if she wrote with left-slanted lower loops before they became friends, she has a complex where sex is concerned that could be at the root of the falling out she mentions and be the reason that she felt unimportant even while being dated.

An adult handwriting with wavy rather than completed loops indicates emotional frustration, as in the sample below. The downstrokes denoting lower loops

*love my family*

are waved, uncrossed. Yet letters slant extremely rightward and the pen pressure is forceful, indicating strong emotional impact. The writer is a seaman who is away from home most' of the time. His emotional drive is a constant hunger that is frustrated for months at a time. Apparently this has destroyed his ability to enjoy his family. His wife describes him as "critical and bad tempered, completely lacking in understanding." She says he is "jealous even of her affection for the children."

*might type*

Double crossed or twisted lower loops indicate sublimation of sex in one who has taken a vow of celibacy. The average person who writes with twisted lower loops suffers from a feeling of unreasonable guilt where sex is concerned. This can be caused by an over-strict parent during the teenage years. Twisting of lower loops when continued after marriage indicates a state of mind that may cause the writer to expiate his or her sense of guilt upon the family in a manner that may appear unreasonable or tyrannical.

Outflung lower loops, as in the *y*'s of Danny Kaye's signature, are an indication of generosity, even altruism.

*The Upper Zone*

In the upper zone, tall loops reach up above the mundane. When full as well as tall, the writer has ingenious ideas and the desire to share his idealism.

Tall narrow upper loops indicate discretion, sometimes shyness ("I am easily hurt").

*You and Your Handwriting*

A delicately pressured writing with tall upper loops reflects idealism, super-sensitivity.

*I have always wanted*

Tall upper loops are usually written with light pen pressure. When tall and written with vigorous pen pressure, the writer has high principles that he insists others respect, especially if letter connectives are angular. The

*my wife was contacted*

man who wrote this note was complaining in his letter about the high-pressure tactics used to induce his wife to sign a contract, and he was writing directly to the company concerned.

When upper loops are so tall that the writing looks unbalanced, the writer may have idealistic illusions. A happy teenager wrote the sample below.

*steady with a wonderful guy.*

*Your Libido* 87

A less happy writer is a man who wrote the following.

*never suspected anything like*

He considered himself ideally married, but discovered his wife has been cheating on him. The emphasis in his writing is upon upper loops. In her writing the accent was upon the lower loops.

Besides the loops, a zone of writing may be accentuated by extraneous strokes. Financier Conrad Hilton accents the lower zone of his writing by curving word endings into the lower zone.

*Conrad Hilton*

*[signature: Debbie Reynolds]*

Debbie Reynolds accents the upper zone with the high-reaching stroke that concludes *Reynolds*.

The chart on page 157 will show you the traits revealed in various shaped loops as affected by slant. A single writing may contain several different loop formations. Each is significant.

# eight
## Social Consciousness

The heart of your handwriting is the middle zone as described in the preceding chapter. You express the essence of your personality in this area, as well as your social consciousness.

You like companionship and you enjoy working with others if your middle zone letters are from medium to large size.

Your thoughts are well-concentrated if you write with small size middle zone letters, and you do not allow yourself to be easily distracted by social demands.

An exaggerated middle zone indicates the wish to impress others with your talents, personality or importance. You may be physically small, yet feel big inside. Tiny opera star Lily Pons writes with high, wide, rounded letters that seem to reach out to enfold her great voice and her great audiences.

*(See next page)*

A capacity for concentrating and organizing is indicated by small, even, middle zone letters. (See J. Edgar Hoover, page 20).

Very small-sized middle zone letters reflect deep absorption in ideas or ideals. Simplified, tiny letters, with low capitals, disclose intellectuality and/or spiritual absorption. Einstein wrote with tiny simplified letters; so did Gandhi; so does President De Gaulle, who once remarked, "Why try to reach the moon? The farthest a man can go is within himself." President De Gaulle is

*President DeGaulle*

*Social Consciousness* 91

effortlessly impressive and does not feel the need of large letters to draw attention.

The size, slant, and formation of strokes should be considered simultaneously. Kate Smith's cordial friendliness is expressed in the wide, right-slanted, garlanded middle zone of her writing.

> Dear Miss Stafford:
> May I be one of
> the first of your fans
> to wish you lots of
> success with your
> new book.
> Kate Smith.

The young lady who wrote the sample "finishing school" also emphasizes the middle zone, but letters are vertical and highly stylized. She is formal, restrained, social rather than sociable. Her letter is from a noted girls' school where manners and propriety take precedence.

*You and Your Handwriting*

Dear Muriel Stafford
    I have just read the handwriting
analysis you did for a friend of mine

Warm generous sociability is expressed in the large, strong-pressured, right-slanted middle zone letters written by Warren Hull.

*Dear Muriel —*

*Good luck with your book*

*Sincerely,*
*Warren Hull*

The size of your letters may vary. You may write with much smaller letters when concentrating upon your work or studies than when you are writing a letter to a friend and your social consciousness is thereby stimulated.

*Social Consciousness* 93

Small, cramped, angular middle zone letters show introversion, and sometimes antagonism, due to self-consciousness, as in the handwriting "I am fat and inclined to be acid-tongued."

*I am fat and inclined to be acid-tongued.*

The writer of "People don't like me. Will you tell me why?" has an unattractive personality for a different reason. The middle zone of her letters is small, rounded, and unslanted. Letters look like tiny caves under which the writer's personality is hidden. She lacks spontaneity and sympathetic interest in others.

*The question is, people don't like me. Will you tell me why?*

Extroversion is evident in a middle zone of exaggerated size. This, too, can be a source of social problems. The girl who wrote "I often wonder why people don't want to be friends with me," writes with very large middle zone letters. Her capitals, too, are oversized. She an-

## 94  *You and Your Handwriting*

tagonizes associates by striving to impress her personality and self-importance upon them.

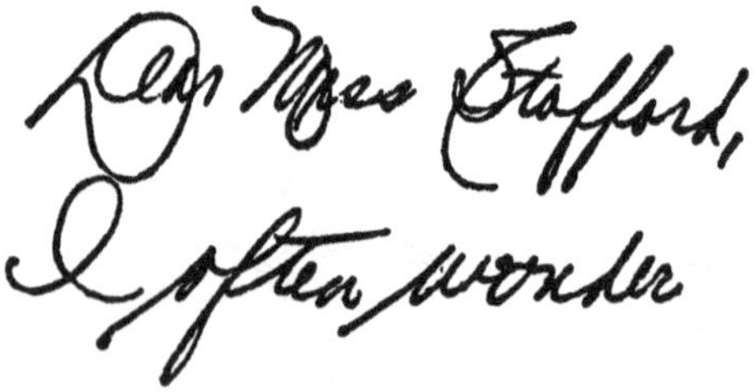

*[handwritten: Dear Mrs Stafford, I often wonder]*

Letters slanted leftward in which the middle zone is emphasized reveals a contradiction of personality. Effusiveness of manner may cover insecurity. The writer enjoys people and can be excellent in contact work, but is inwardly wary. His cordial manner attracts, but he may not believe that others really like him and may suspect that his friends are merely using him.

*[handwritten: Do let me hear]*

"The sign of the perfect host" is the term applied to a word in which the middle zone dwindles in height with the last letter of the word lowest, as in President Eisenhower's signature. Maturity of thought, diplomacy, and charm are thus indicated. (This dwindling of letter size is very apparent throughout the handwriting of the Duchess of Windsor.)

*Social Consciousness* 95

*[signature: Dwight D. Eisenhower]*

Irregular height of middle zone letters indicates versatility when letters are well-developed, as in Mrs. Roosevelt's signature.

*[signature: Eleanor Roosevelt]*

When letters are poorly developed, however, a very irregular middle zone may reveal a jack-of-all-trades because of his incapacity to settle down.

A middle zone that gradually increases in height so that the last letter becomes highest denotes gullibility, sometimes wishful thinking. In the signature of Premier Tito, the large garlands indicate a cordial showman, but the middle zone becomes gradually higher so that the *o* is highest.

*[signature: Tito]*

## 96  *You and Your Handwriting*

The descriptive letters that follow combine middle zone indications with slant, shape, and pressure. More than one letter could refer to your writing.

*note was written*

*I think I have succeeded*

*I discovered your column*

*know who had the most*

## Social Consciousness

*and will continue to*

*seem enough times*

*I even hate a compliment*

*referred me to you*

*compatible person*

*thank you very much*

*Face the run*

*writing samples*

*analysis of my writing*

I prefer a heavy pen


always been fascinated

# nine

## *Your State of Mind, Health and Nerves*

Middle zone letters are written upon an invisible line from left to right termed in graphology the "baseline." The direction of this baseline and its steadiness across the page reflect your state of mind and vitality. Basic character traits are also denoted by the steadiness of this line.

A baseline so straight that all the middle zone letters appear to be written on a drawn line denotes a sincere and forthright character. Conscientiousness is emphasized by small size letters of even height written on a very steady baseline.

*me. A large portion of my work — ting and typing of theses, dissertatio intific textbooks, articles for public-*

A straight baseline can be an affectation, however, if the handwriting itself appears artificial, overstylized, as in the sample, "He is very erratic." The writer wishes to *appear* sincere and forthright.

*He is very erratic*

The disturbed, uneven baseline in the sample "I mean things I do never please her" reflects emotional instability and insecurity. The writer's low *I* indicates that his sense of inferiority contributes to this state of mind. Frequent garlands stress his desire to be obliging, but he is also critical, nervous, supersensitive. Angularity is pronounced at the top and at the base of letter *m* in the word *mean*.

*I mean things I do never please her—*

A wavy baseline indicates a moody disposition, as illustrated in the baseline of "anxious girl." She wants very much to be married and might be better able to achieve her aim if she could stabilize her disposition.

*(See next page)*

> *At twenty-five what I want most is marriage*

A slightly upslanted baseline indicates vitality of mind and body. When extremely upslanted, very high optimism is indicated.

A downslanted baseline may have one of several causes. Most small children write with a downslant because they tire so quickly.

In an adult writing, downslanted lines of writing reveal weariness, dejection, and/or low vitality. When lines of writing become increasingly downslanted toward the bottom of the page, either sinking strength or else an increasing sense of depression is revealed. When the downslant of line is caused by a temporary state of mind, the writer may conclude the page with a more cheerful slant of the baseline.

Lines that become increasingly downslanted, with unsteady strokes, reveal increasing weariness and low vitality.

Temporarily downslanted letters can be caused by bad news, as in the handwriting of Cordell Hull. (See page 58.)

If each word in a line of writing is downslanted, yet every word begins higher than the last letter of the preceding word, the writer doesn't give in easily. He always

## Your State of Mind, Health and Nerves 103

"comes back for more." This struggle against discouragement is shown in the handwriting, "Better in an apartment by myself." The writer is living with her married daughter but knows in her heart that the situation is inadvisable, though she tries to keep her chin up and make the best of things.

*Better in an apartment by myself*

When a line of writing ascends towards the center of the page but dips down at the end, the writer is by nature optimistic and feels low due to some current circumstance.

A baseline that dips in the center reveals recent unhappiness from which the writer is gradually recovering. The first time I noticed such a baseline as a graphologist and asked the writer if she had been recently unhappy, she replied softly, "My baby died last week."

Be sure when analyzing baseline that the paper was in normal alignment with the writer's arm. If the paper is overslanted, the direction of the baseline can be misleading. An unnatural baseline can also result from an unnatural writing position.

The lines that say "This is something I've wanted to do for a long time" show an upslant in the first line as the writer thinks with optimistic anticipation. By the second line, she remembers her problem, and that line slants downward. In her letter, the writer said, "This is something I've wanted to do for a long time. I'm very anxious to know what you can tell after studying my

## 104  *You and Your Handwriting*

handwriting. I'm 25 years old, married, and the mother of 5 children.

"I love my husband and consider being a wife and mother a very worthwhile way to spend a lifetime. But for some reason I'm somewhat unhappy and terribly over-anxious. The tranquillizers my doctor has prescribed don't seem to help too much. I thought perhaps you could give me a few of the answers I'm looking for."

*This is something I've wanted to do for a long*

The writer is worrisome and introverted, according to her tiny, pinched letters, but that upslanted first line indicates that she has a capacity for being interested and optimistic. She should find an outlet for her intensely concentrated mind and perhaps her lines of writing will slant upward again.

The baseline may be downslanted in one particular line or paragraph, with the remainder of the lines on the page upslanted. If so, the writer may have been depressed by the thoughts that occurred as the downslanted lines were being written or by the incident being related. To follow the trend of a baseline in the handwriting of a sensitive writer is sometimes like following his emotional path.

The lines "God bless you all, Mom" conclude a page of writing that began with a baseline that went straight across the page. Gradually the lines of writing became more and more downslanted, and these concluding lines reveal a very low vitality, not only in the extreme downslant of letters but also in the shakiness of strokes. Low-

*Your State of Mind, Health and Nerves* 105

er loops were fully formed at the top of the page, but weakness contributes to the unformed lower loop in *y*.

*God bless you all*
*Mom*

Dejection rather than low vitality is revealed in the downslant of lines in the writing that speaks of suicide ("several months ago," etc.).

*but a few months ago,*
*I tried to commit suicide,*
*n't even do anything*

The writer of "no one else seems to be able" is overcoming her dejection. The line dips in the center but turns up again at the end.

*no one else seems to be able*

# ten
## *Approach and Conclusion*

Your manner of approach, your maturity of character, and your mental alertness are expressed in the way you begin words.

During your first years in school, you may have learned to write each word with a little preliminary stroke. As you became increasingly confident, you gradually began to eliminate these strokes, and now you may use very few, if any. A direct, quick mind tends to simplify words and letters so as not to halt pen motion.

Some writers, however, start each word with a preliminary upstroke even though they were not taught to do so in school. This elaboration is significant. An upstroke at the beginning of a word is somewhat like the motion of a hand in its implications. The stroke may seem to cling to the line as if grasping for balance (dependency, unsureness), or push vigorously upward, away from the line, indicating aggressiveness. Sometimes a beginning stroke, like a willful child, both clings and pushes assertively.

## Approach and Conclusion   107

Long beginning strokes combined with undeveloped letter forms, indicate immaturity. This does not refer to chronological age, which cannot be established through handwriting, but to the development of character and abilities.

A young man twenty years of age wrote this. His ungainly letters are unsteadily formed. Beginning strokes in

*soon as possible*

this writing curve along the line, then push upward assertively. The writer demonstrated willfulness by insisting upon immediate marriage though his fiancée thought they should wait until he had graduated from college or had established himself in a position. Though he got his way, he was not ready for responsibility and independence. During the three months after his marriage, he quit two jobs, left his wife and returned to his mother's home, at which time he wrote this specimen.

The young man who wrote "to arrive at your place in the" was also twenty years of age but the handwriting shows maturity and high intelligence. Letters are simplified, swiftly written, with discarded beginning strokes. Loops that begin a word are replaced by a straight line so that the writer can begin with a downstroke instead of an upstroke. This young man at the time he wrote was concluding his fourth year of college in preparation for medical school and had been on the honor roll all the way through college.

*(See next page)*

*to arrive at your place*

Long beginning strokes may be an expression of resentment as well as aggressiveness. "I have worked" was written by a wife who stated at length that she had contributed more than her share to her marriage and felt that her efforts were not appreciated.

*I have worked*

Sometimes a young person's handwriting will reflect more emotional maturity than a parent's, as in a comparison of the two writings here. The mother (SHE) begins her first word with a curved stroke like a greeting wave of the hand. A good sense of humor and a love of fun are indicated. However, most of her words begin

*Now tell me why my*

She

*Approach and Conclusion* 109

with an upstroke. In the letter she wrote, she gaily derided her daughter.

Her daughter's writing, reproduced beneath hers, is formed of small, carefully formed, rounded letters—left-slanted! Words show neither beginning nor ending strokes. She is a bright, serious girl with much reserve. The left-slant of her letters may be due to a feeling of defensiveness because of her mother's constant teasing.

*I am fourteen years old*

*Daughter*

A swift, creative mind is likely to discard all beginning strokes as in the distinctive handwriting of playwright Thornton Wilder. His heavy pen pressure reveals an impressive will and personality but independence of thought and action. (See page 21).

The ending stroke of your words discloses your manner of conclusion, whether brief, abrupt, persistent, or determined. Ending strokes of words also reflect the writer's personality.

You may increase the length of your word endings and the strength of pen pressure towards the conclusion of a note, as does Thornton Wilder in his signature. Most of his word endings are brief, although the pressure at the end of a word always deepens. As he comes to "Cordially," the concluding stroke lengthens, thickens. His signature ends with a long, forceful straight line, indicating determined perseverance.

110   *You and Your Handwriting*

Occasionally a single word shows a significantly forceful word ending. The word on which it appears may be significant as in "I feel she detests me." The word "she" ends with a long, straight stroke. A mother was referring to her young daughter whom she felt did not love her.

*I feel she detests me*

No other word in the mother's letter ends in a straight line, and her handwriting shows an inherently kind and charming personality. I suggested to her that she might be neglecting to use her charm on her daughter and that the daughter might feel that all her mother wanted was to make her obey. "In fact she may think that you detest her!" I told the mother. She wrote later to thank me and to say that she had changed her attitude towards her daughter and the situation had changed completely.

Brief word endings are a simplification denoting a quick mind, but when the ending is so abrupt that the last letter is not fully formed as in three words of "as soon as possible," the writer is hasty, quits before completion, lacks perseverance.

*since we are so close*

Word endings that curl back over the word are a "return to self," denoting introversion. In "since we are so close" these are emphasized by several indications of a

## Approach and Conclusion   111

withdrawn nature including letters *a* and *o* tied at the top with a little knot, also left-slanted letters and an i-dot formed as a circle. The writer shut herself away and then wondered why she was lonely. She had recently married and felt she should know her husband better "since we are so close." Actually, her husband's writing indicated an affectionate, responsive, outgoing nature. She did not seem to realize that she, herself, raised the barriers.

In considering personality traits as revealed by word endings, remember the rules for connectives. Pointed word endings show aggressiveness, temper ("arrangements"). Those that curve over in an arcade indicate reserve and protectiveness ("Thanking"). A softly upcurved stroke at the end of a word indicates an obliging nature, as does the garland ("successful in"). When two or three letters are replaced by a thread at the end of a word, a swift, creative mind is revealed if the writing as a whole is simplified, graceful, as in "Thanking you again."

*Thanking you again*

Your knowledge of the significance of "zones" may also be used in analyzing word endings. Those that aspire into the upper zone indicate an idealistic, high-minded person ("analysis"). When word endings persistently finish beneath the line, the writer is materialistic ("push").

*analysis*

*push*

# eleven
*Headlining Your Personality*

Your capitals are the headlines in a page of your handwriting. Each is analyzed according to its individual formation and also in proportion to the other letters.

Large, flourished capitals shout, "Here comes important news—Me!" This may or may not be true, depending on the quality of the handwriting. You may be more important news if your capitals are simply formed and of moderate height, reflecting mental absorption rather than the urge to make an impression.

The headlines may be misleading if there is a strong contradiction between the size or formation of capitals versus other letters. For instance, exaggerated capitals lead one to expect an expansive personality, but when combined with undersized small letters, they are a mask. The expansion is all on the surface. The writer is more serious, shy, or worrisome than he allows himself to appear.

*(See next page)*

*[handwritten: Dear Muriel]*

When the capitals that refer to the writer are expanded (*I* and the initials of his signature) but the initial letter of another's name is minimized, the connotation is an exploitation of self. In this note from Frank Sinatra, the words are flattering, but the size of the initial in the word "Muriel" is quite the opposite!

*[handwritten: Dear Muriel— I think you're wonderful. Frank Sinatra]*

Capital *M* is an exceptionally expressive capital since it consists of three downstrokes and two or three connective strokes.

Besides, there is always a capital letter *M* in the salutary line of each of the hundreds of thousands of re-

*Headlining of Your Personality* 115

quests I receive for analyses. Written by another, *M* in "Muriel" says "You!" The formation may be consistent throughout the writing, or each *M* may have another story to tell. Variations are all significant.

A complex writer may disclose a range of traits in a single letter *M*. In "Muriel," written by Dean Acheson when he was Secretary of State, *M* is small, wide, left-slanted, and simplified, denoting an intellectual introvert. The first stroke becomes a guarded arcade followed by an angular connective (critical, analytical), then a garland (cordiality).

*Miss Muriel Stafford*
*a sample of my*
*hand writing*
*Dean Acheson*

A left slant of the first stroke of *M*, contradicted later by a right slant, indicates preliminary wariness; but when the letters that follow slant rightward the writer soon lets down the bars. This combination is shown in the word "Muriel" written by Clark Gable, whom I had just met at the time he wrote. Although the first stroke is left-slanted and comes down to an angular base, the

*M* closes with the cordial u-shaped motion garland. The small letters are warmly right-slanted.

As *I* reflects both the writer's self-image and his true personality traits, so to a certain extent does the manner in which he writes the *M* in "Muriel" give me a hint of how he rates me in comparison to himself.

*Dear Muriel
Hope you can
read it.
Clark Gable*

*Headlining of Your Personality* 117

*Variations of Capital M*

Straight downstroke. *by Bill Holden*

A direct, alert mind.

Gracefully waved. *by Ted Williams*

Gay, genial, sense of humor.

Pointed. *by Cary Grant*

Independent, assertive.

118  *You and Your Handwriting*

Large incurve. *by Janis Paige*

Hidden thoughts, often secret sorrow.

Retraced. *by Arlene Frances*

Guarded, discreet.

Extremely rightward. *by Ingrid Bergman*

Deeply emotional, sensitive.

*Headlining of Your Personality* 119

*Muriel*

Extremely leftward.         *by Keenan Wynn*

Sense of rejection, emotional repression.

*Muriel*

Vertical.         *by Garry Moore*

Self-reliant, level-headed.

*Muriel,*

All humps rounded.         *by Richard Widmark*

Reserved, good-natured.

*Muriel*

All humps pointed.          *by Douglas Fairbanks, Jr.*

Keenly analytical.

*Muriel*

W-shaped.          *by Steve Allen*

Obliging, likable.

Printed or simplified in a unique way.      *by Fanny Hurst*

Creative talent (art, music, literature, or drama).

*Headlining of Your Personality* 121

Heart-shaped. *by Frankie Laine*

Romantic self-presentation.

*Miss*

Moderate size, conventional shape. *by Kate Smith*

Normal ego, unpretentious.

*Muriel!*

Very large. *by Joe E. Brown*

Extrovert, instinctive showman.

*Miss*

Small, low. *By Bradford Dillman*

Modest approach.

*Muriel*

Gracefully elaborated. *by Joan Fontaine*

Creative, attention-compelling.

*Muriel*

Exaggerated and overelaborated. *by Carmen Miranda*

Love of gaudy display.

*Headlining of Your Personality*   123

*muriel*

All humps level height.  *by Sid Caesar*

    Stubborn will, sometimes not apparent.

*Muriel*

Third hump highest.  *by Jack Benny*

    Set convictions, resistant to pressure.

*M uriel*

Thick, heavy strokes.  *by Gregory Peck*

    Compelling, magnetic.

# twelve
## *Eloquent Strokes*

Your handwriting is not static but alive—moving, variable in the ways you are variable. Nowhere is this more apparent than in the way the stem of *t* is crossed or not crossed. A t-bar may stress traits otherwise evident in a handwriting or may show traits otherwise unrevealed.

A single writing may show many variations of the t-bar. Each is significant. If all the bars are similar, consistency is indicated as regards whatever traits the bar reveals.

A woman once handed me a sheet of paper with every t-bar long, heavy, thickening in pressure like a little club, yet she had written, "Forgiveness is a divine trait."

"Forgiveness is a divine trait but not one of yours," I replied. "How did you happen to write this quotation?"

She answered, "My sister-in-law wrote it in a letter I got this morning." She paused. "I haven't spoken to her for twenty years." Another pause. "I'm not going to, either!" she concluded.

Meaningless quotations such as, "Now is the time for all good men to come to the aid of their party" are not advisable as samples for analysis because the mind is not stimulated by the words being written. The aforementioned quotation, however, was a good sample for analysis because the words stirred the writer so deeply.

A t-bar may be strikingly similar to other horizontal strokes in the same writing as in "writings all in." This t-bar is a long graceful stroke ending in a little curve and the word "in" concludes with a similar stroke. Even the dash between words is similar.

Heavier pressure at the beginning of a t-bar indicates force of will that diminishes in strength. A deepening of pressure at the end of a t-bar denotes a will that perseveres. The lady who had held a grudge for twenty years used her perseverance and stubborn determination in a negative way, illustrating that how a trait is used may determine whether it is "good" or "bad."

A long firm bar denotes a sense of responsibility and good will power. A single t-bar may cross two t's with a single stroke, as illustrated in the word "interesting" in the handwriting of Thomas E. Dewey, or may connect two words ("letter of"). A logical, fluent mind is indicated by the connection of words.

*(See next page)*

Dear Miss Stafford:
          I have just received
your letter of March 6 and
am happy to send you
another — more up-to-date
specimen of handwriting for
your delightful — and piercing,
analysis.
          With kindest personal
regards and best wishes to
you in your interesting work,
                    Sincerely yours,
                    Thomas S. Derey

Mar. 7, 1944.

The "ups and downs" of t-bars are significant. An upslanted bar aspires, denoting ambition. ("present day writing") Downslanted t-bars reveal dictatorial impulses, sometimes not realized by the writer and often due to a buried hurt.

*present day writing*

A high t-bar shows imagination and a low bar a practical "down-to-earth" attitude. If the bar is so high that it does not touch the stem, quick temper is reflected.

*you think in time*

When no t-bar is used, absentmindedness is indicated. Weakly written t-bars show weakness of will.

A t-bar should not be analyzed without considering the writing as a whole. A short, firm bar in a neat writing shows carefulness. This may refer to surface appearances if letters are written with fussy precision ("fascinated").

*fascinated*

## 128  *You and Your Handwriting*

The t-bars in the handwriting of J. Edgar Hoover (page 20) are also short and precisely placed and his writing is clear, simplified, evenly spaced. His mind is careful and exact.

Thomas E. Dewey also writes with many short, firm bars. His writing tends towards angularity and a variation of letter forms as well as many kinds of t-bars. He combines mental exactness with versatility.

*How about this one?*

Hooks cling. Points dig. A tiny hook on a t-bar (or word ending) indicates persistence ("How about this one"). Knotlike t-bars are another indication of tenacity. A sarcastic retort may be expected when t-bars come to a sharp point like tiny daggers.

The absence of an indication in a writing does not necessarily mean that the writer lacks the quality that would accompany that formation. Nowhere can this be better illustrated than with t-bars. For instance, an upslanted t-bar denotes ambition, but if your t-bars do not point upwards, that does not mean that you therefore lack ambition. This rule is not merely for t-bars. A handwriting must be analyzed only according to what is actually there.

*I try to be*

*Eloquent Strokes* 129

*don't always let it*

A t-bar placed on the left without crossing the bar as in "I try to b," denotes procrastination, frustration.

A henpecked husband wrote, "I don't think it's fair" in which the t-bars are not only weak but placed mostly

*I don't think it fair*

on the left side of the stem, reflecting his expressed sense of frustration.

The t-bars in "wanting this other than" are also on the left of the stem but they are written with strong pressure and slant downward, demonstrating frustration plus resentment.

*wanting this other than*

A t-bar placed mostly (or all) on the right side of the stem reveals assertiveness, as in the second word of "without interfering." The word "without" shows an equal amount of bar before and after the stem of *t*, but as she wrote the second word the writer felt more aggressive. The urge to express herself is likely to cause this writer to "interfere" even though she says she does not wish to do so. Thus does our writing sometimes contradict our words.

*without interfering*

A t-bar crossed by an ending stroke as in "write pretty" is a back-to-self motion symbolizing the writer's concentration upon himself and his own problems.

*I can, and pretty well*

We seldom consider the way we dot an *i*. An i-dot is easy to overlook when analyzing a handwriting. Of course there are exceptions, like the symbolic heart-shaped i-dots used by Jayne Mansfield that make her writing look like a sentimental valentine (See page 36).

The rules for placement given for t-bars also apply to i-dots. A high dot indicates imagination, a low dot a practical mind. When exactly over the stem, carefulness is stressed. Hesitancy is shown when placed before the stem, and action when the i-dot follows the stem. Wariness is expressed in very low i-dots placed exactly over the stem. The writer who completely neglects i-dots is absentminded or careless about nonessential details.

A slightly curved i-dot, like a waved t-bar, shows a fun-loving nature but a full circle i-dot emphasizes in-

*Eloquent Strokes* 131

troversion and a flair for the artistic. You will find circle i-dots most frequently in a writing that shows other indications of introversion, such as curled back word endings, sometimes a left slant of letters.

A v-shaped dot is an indication of an analytical mind (Thomas E. Dewey, page 126: "with," "in"). A dot made with heavy pen pressure is an expression of a dominating will (Duchess of Windsor, Warren Hull, Chapters 5 and 8).

A heavy, slashing i-dot, made like a dagger, is an indication of brutality.

The letter *g* made with an unhalted graceful motion so that it resembles the numeral *8* accents the writer's cultural tastes. So does the small letter *e* when occasionally formed like a reversed *3* (the Greek *e*). These two formations are illustrated in the handwriting of Clare Booth Luce. Her handwriting is highly simplified with many indications of creative literary talent, including the "literary" *d* (formed with an upstroke but no loop).

A small letter *r*, written with ultra-precision, indicates an observant eye and the ability to notice and remember details of surface appearances. In an extremely neat handwriting, an overfussy *r* indicates a perfectionist.

An *r* that seems to rear above the other letters is, to put it succinctly, an indication of snobbery. This may be found in surprising places. "Striking handwriting" was written by a college boy who belonged to a very exclusive fraternity. The letters *r* rise conspicuously.

*Striking handwriting*

"Dear Muriel" was written by a young lady whose vocation has a snob appeal; the staging of high-class fashion shows. She, too, rears the letter *r*.

*Dear Muriel*

The small letter *m* is also exceptionally eloquent. Consider *m* according to the rules for capital *M* as illustrated in the chapter "Headlining Your Personality."

# thirteen
*Vocational Aptitudes*

The wife of a noted surgeon once handed me two completely different handwritings for analysis. The first was written with undeveloped letters of medium size. The second writing was small-lettered, energetic, with clear, simplified, rather angular forms. The lady disconcerted me by saying, "My husband wrote them both!" Then she smiled and said, "He was eighteen years old when he wrote the first."

Aptitude is developed through training and experience, so don't despair if your handwriting does not yet indicate your capacity for a vocation that is your ambition. As you learn and develop your capacities, your writing will change.

An industrious and competent worker with a logical mind is indicated by clear, small-lettered handwriting with letters of a word carefully connected.

*(See next page)*

*free-lance secretarial work*

A less industrious and competent worker is revealed in "job as a secretary." Sloppy letters of uncondensed size waver uncertainly. The young lady wrote a plaintive letter in which she complains that her boss "seems very particular" and is disappointed because she is not faster; also "the earpiece on the dictaphone is always falling off." She asks "what would you suggest?" Frankly, not a secretarial position.

*job as secretary*

Her large rounded middle zone letters indicate that this writer would be best in a position where she would be in contact with people, but not in a position requiring too much attention to detail, since her writing is not meticulous in any way.

Those who write with large simplified letters enjoy the stage, promotional work, or some similar field.

Desi Arnaz was a young bandleader when I analyzed his handwriting. He wrote with impressive, simplified letters and high, printed capitals. He combined angular letters with the suavity of a garlanded signature.

"You'd make an excellent actor, better still, a producer," I told him.

A few years afterwards, Desi became a producer of TV films. The series, "I Love Lucy," in which he acted as leading man as well as producer and director, was a sensational success. He set up his own company, demonstrating his business ability.

> Dear Muriel:
> What can I say in two lines, eh?
>
> Desi Arnaz

Here's a warning for you if you write with large letters and high flourished capitals. You are so well able to sell yourself that you may obtain positions that you soon find boring and tedious. You like variety, plenty of companionship, and you do not like to be tied down to monotonous routine.

If you write with tiny letters, you are industrious and smart, but if letters are pinched, you may also be shy and worrisome. Remember to smile when you are being interviewed for a position or you may not get the chance to demonstrate your excellent abilities.

Training in a specialized profession might cause the size of your letters to condense. If you already write with small letters, you are well suited for a position that requires intensity of thought and attention to details. If your small-sized letters are well-spaced and steadily written, your employer will find you invaluable. You may be so efficient that your employer will decide you should be promoted to a management position. Make sure that your handwriting includes indications of executive ability or you may find the promotion is not to your advantage.

A business house once gave me a handwriting for analysis without telling me anything about the writer except these three facts: (1) He had been an assistant to one of the top officials. (2) He was promoted. (3) Soon afterwards they had to fire him. The question was, "What caused him to be successful in his original position with the company yet incompetent when promoted?" His handwriting was small, meticulous, low-capitaled, with weak t-bars. The middle zone letters were cramped. His writing indicates that under supervision he would be industrious, but he had no talent for handling others. When the personnel manager read the analysis of this man's handwriting, he remarked, "Too bad. If we'd had this done two years ago, we'd still have a valuable employee—and he'd have a job."

The handwriting of Thomas E. Dewey (see page 126), former Governor of the State of New York and a candidate for the United States Presidency, illustrates a well-concentrated mind and professional proficiency combined with executive ability and a decisive will. His letters are low, narrow, with discarded excess strokes. He writes energetically, with t-bars that are sometimes short and concise and at other times long—but always firm in pressure. His signature, written as one word without lifting the pen, emphasizes his executive ability.

Rounded letters disclose an urge to cover or protect. An architect protects with a house. An insurance salesman protects with insurance. A nurse protects the sick. A mother protects her children. Whatever your vocation may be, from a kindergarten teacher to an officer of the law, if you round your letters you enjoy the protective role afforded by your vocation.

*I am a nurse who*

*not like to live in New York*

With the right training, those who make angular letters may excel in law, research, engineering, medicine, electronics, and other specialized professions requiring critical concentration. Increased regularity of size and spacing as well as smaller-sized letters is usually the result of the training that lifts a man from a mechanic to an engineer. The writer of "not like to live in New York" is an engineer.

If you can sell, you have a golden key to financial success. Employers have different ideas about the qualities they want in a salesman, but there are some qualities that none of them want, including laziness, dishonesty, instability, timidity, and poor health.

A handwriting that is messy and confused, with lines of writing that overlap, will tell the employer that, at best, he cannot expect accurate reports, and, at worst, that he is sending a man as his representative who is muddleheaded and unreliable as regards details.

Initiative and drive are indicated by vigorously written letters, especially if they are somewhat angular and pen pressure strong.

A subtle salesman whose handwriting reveals a talent for the right word at the right time will not need so much aggression.

Printed capitals and simplification that includes the disconnection of some letters in a single word show an intuitive mind, and the writer has strong hunches. If his letters slant rightward, he is inclined to act upon them immediately. If letters slant leftward, he analyzes his hunch carefully before going ahead. This writer may also have a gift for leading a person to an idea and making that person think it was his own.

A steady flow of letters and consistent slant indicate good mental and emotional control. When letters look shaken, irregular, with a markedly unsteady baseline,

## Vocational Aptitudes 139

the writer's nerves may betray him no matter how hard he tries. If your own handwriting fits this description and you find everyone very annoying, see a doctor. You may be like the woman who said to her doctor after taking tranquillizers for a while: "No, I haven't changed. It's just that people are so much nicer."

A wider variation of handwritings appears among successful actors and actresses than in any other profession. Some stars are extroverts who have sought the stage to display their personalities. Others are introverts. Henry Fonda's handwriting, for instance, is small-lettered, left-slanted. I said to him, "How did you ever happen to become an actor? You dislike to display your feelings!" He replied, "I feel when I go on the stage as if I am wearing a mask and nobody can see me behind that mask."

There are other reasons that the stage seems desirable to so many different kinds of people. The rewards are rich, and the handwriting of an actor who exaggerates lower zone loops shows that the opportunity to make big money is a strong factor in his choice of vocation. The "money-bag" lower loop is frequent amongst successful actors. (see Mason, Durante, Chapters 6 and 7).

Whatever your qualities may be, use them in the vocation of your choice. The greater the need for your particular traits, the more successful you will be in your work.

# fourteen
## *Making Your Mark*

Your signature is exclusively yours. Thousands may share your name, but when you write your signature, the particular John Jones who is YOU becomes identified so clearly that even a stranger will honor your check or credit card.

As you develop mentally and emotionally your signature too gradually develops, and the new person who is you cannot use out-of-date identification.

Your signature is the essence of your personality. Traits indicated throughout your writing are almost sure to be indicated in your signature, and more. If you elaborate capitals because of vanity, the initial letters of your signature will also be elaborated—unless of course you are trying to conceal your feeling of self-importance. If you are creative, your signature will reflect your talent.

The force of pen pressure in your signature indicates how forcefully you strive to assert yourself. The strength of pressure may be modified with indications of diplo-

*[signature: Harold Macmillan]*

macy and tact, however, as in the handwriting of Prime Minister Macmillan.

President Delano Roosevelt (1940) also wrote with decisiveness and speed. Right-slanted, severely trimmed, unconnected downstrokes lean rightward, thickening at the base. Swift intuition is combined with unhesitating force of will. Though connective strokes between the small letters are discarded, capital *D* swings directly into capital *R,* an indication of executive ability in a signature.

*[signature: Franklin D. Roosevelt]*

*The White House*
*January 24, 1936*

A comparison of the way you write your given name with the initial of your family name denotes whether you feel inferior or superior to your family. A tall first name shows confidence in yourself, but if overexaggerated, as in the handwriting of Fidel Castro, self-glorification is revealed. Fidel Castro's last name is "Ruz." Here the word "Ruz" is neglected and disguised. Over-

*Fidel Castro*

attention elaborates the given name "Fidel." The connection between the words of this signature is most unusual. The last letter of "Fidel" becomes the first letter of "Castro" by the simple expedient of stabbing $l$ with a rapid motion of the pen. The word "Fidel" is thereby stabbed in the back. This could indicate suicidal impulses. The urge to commit suicide is, in some cases, expiated by the killing of another person (or persons).

In contrast to Castro's overemphasized signature capitals, upper zone, revealing his desire for personal acclaim, Nikita Khrushchev writes with a signature that is completely in the "middle zone," giving no attention to the upper zone, even in his initials. Neither is the lower zone recognized. His "social consciousness" is all-absorbing. He has neither spiritual aspirations nor confidence in his personal prestige. Wide garlanded connective

*Nikita Khrushchev*

strokes indicate that Khrushchev possesses a genial charm but with so little confidence in his own importance he feels that to impress VIP's it is necessary for him to make extravagant boasts and threats, even at the expense of his dignity—as when he banged the desk with his shoe at the United Nations.

Madam Khrushchev also writes with a strongly accented middle zone, but in her signature the upper and lower zones are modestly recognized.

Daughter Julia did not suffer for her social consciousness as much as did her parents. This may be why all zones are balanced in her signature, none overemphasized.

As you can see, even written in an unrecognizable language, a signature is eloquent and individualistic—and most rules of graphology are applicable.

The signature of Ben-Gurion in Hebrew is written with swift, emphatic simplicity. The middle zone dwindles gradually in the manner that indicates diplomacy and "the perfect host." The underline beneath his name

*Ben-Gurion*

is an emphasis that draws attention to himself, as are all underlines beneath a signature. This underscore is graciously curved, with a tiny hook at the end, denoting perseverance.

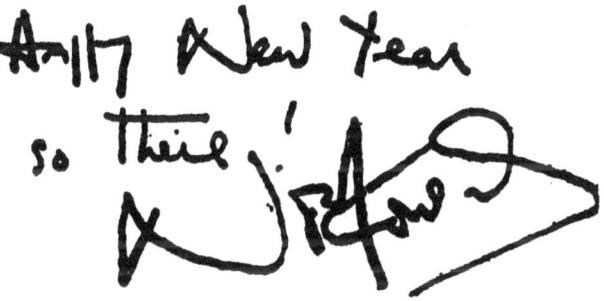

A designed signature that minimizes or completely discards letter forms indicates a swift, creative mind and an enigmatic personality.

What causes a signature to change sharply? A frequent reason is a revision of self-estimate. Sudden spec-

## 146  *You and Your Handwriting*

tacular success, especially on the stage or screen, may stimulate the writer's ego.

The day singer Connie Francis wrote this note she was having photos taken in the gown she was to wear the following Wednesday at a command performance for Queen Elizabeth. Her songs were also topping the hit parade at the time. Self-dramatization and a feeling of high prestige are reflected in the tall flourished capitals of her signature contrasting with her low-capitaled signature before she became so acclaimed.

*Dear Muriel*

*Why has my signature changed from*

*Connie Francis*

*to*

*Connie Francis?*

You may discover that you sometimes write your signature initials high and at other times low. You will discover, if you check, that when capitals are exaggerated in height you are feeling important and sure of yourself, and vice versa.

*Making Your Mark* 147

A clear-lettered, well-spaced signature is an indication of sincerity and a factual mind. An illegible signature indicates an original, creative mind and/or a certain evasiveness.

Doctors, whose profession requires so much diplomacy and discretion, are noted for the illegibility of their signatures. Many politicians and diplomats and some businessmen write their names with indefinable letters.

A change towards extreme signature illegibility may indicate that the writer is under pressure in a position requiring nimble wit and ready answers. Such a change is noticeable in the signature of Pierre Salinger, who wrote a much more legible signature in 1960. After he had been White House Press Secretary for two years and gone through the pressure of the Cuban crisis as intermediary to the press for President Kennedy, his signature dissolved to a swift, curved line indicating gracious elusiveness.

*Pierre Salinger*

*You and Your Handwriting*

You can use graphology to determine the true nature of a person with whom you have business dealings. Just his signature will tell you how to take him and what to expect.

For instance, the signature "David M. Goodstein" is large-sized with clear-cut letters. Charm is emphasized by the wide garlanded "M." This is a man you would like at once. He would treat you fairly, cordially and listen with patience to what you have to say.

You might feel he likes you so much that you can make him agree to anything you propose . . . but notice that his expansive signature is restrained by unslanted letters and the letter "o" is tied at the top with a discreet little knot. Restraint, caution, a level regard for all considerations are indicated. This writer can't be bluffed and he can't be rushed or emotionally impelled. For best results, lay all the facts on the line and make sure they are all accurate. He'll spot any flaws, even if he does not mention them.

*Making Your Mark* 149

Another man may seem antagonistic yet in reality be more susceptible and receptive to your demands and wishes . . . if you handle him with regard to the hints given to you by his handwriting.


Watch your signature as it develops or changes and you can better understand and appreciate yourself.

Mary Martin told me "I distinctly remember four different signatures that I have used at different times in the past. I'll show you." The changes and developments in Mary's personality are vividly reflected in the four contrasting signatures.

*[signature: Mary Martin]*

The first was written as a child. An insecure, reserved personality is evident in the low capitaled left-slanted letters of signature #1. ("I was a mouse!" Mary said.)

*[signature: Mary Martin]*

Sample #2 looks artificial rather than spontaneous. The large, stylized letters indicate a desire to be noticed and admired. ("I was in high school. Just beginning to strut my stuff. I remember writing my name this way because I liked the way it looked," said Mary.)

*Mary Martin*

The small-sized middle zone in Mary Martin's signature #3 reveals concentration of thought and organizing ability. I told Mary that many teachers write similarly and she replied "I was teaching dancing at the time."

*Mary Martin*

Last is her present day signature; assured, dramatic, self-assertive. The two point capital "M" stresses creative talent. The stubborn resolution that has helped towards her success is reflected in the high second bar of "M" and the strong down-slanted "t-bar."

You will find that if you keep an eye on the signatures of the members of your family you can get a good slant on how they feel and the particular need of each. A youngster who begins to sign his name with low-capitaled, narrow-lettered AND left-slanted letters has been ego-injured and he needs your reassurance and love.

A wife whose signature becomes downslanted and weak-stroked is overtired and discouraged with herself. She needs a rest and more consideration from the members of her family.

A husband whose signature becomes angular, jerky, and unsteady will act nervous and critical because he is tensed up. A doctor can help him and it's better to take him to a doctor than to quarrel with him because arguing will make him worse.

That teen-ager whose signature slants too far to the right may be more susceptible than you realize . . . and also supersensitive, so watch your voice and words.

A knowledge of graphology will be a help to you socially, in business or in the accomplishment of a harmonious home. How can you learn the rules? Read carefully and PRACTICE on all your friends and acquaintances. This will not only help you to remember and coordinate the rules but also make you the most sought-after member of any party. You will startle others with your insight and yourself with your new understanding.

# Charts

### USE THIS CHART LIKE A TIMETABLE

1. ACROSS THE TOP, find your correct letter slant.
2. ON THE LEFT SIDE, find the words that best describe your pen pressure.
3. At the place that slant and pressure converge is a description of you.

## THE PRESSURE OF YOUR PEN

| PRESSURE | RIGHT SLANT | VERTICAL OR LEFT SLANT | MIXED SLANT |
|---|---|---|---|
| FAINT | Ultra-sensitive, suggestible, lack of assurance. | Fearful, on the defensive. | Indecisive, need for reassurance, help. |
| LIGHT | Compliant. Sympathetic. Responsive. Seeks approval. | Coolly unresponsive. Aloof. | Conflict. Need for guidance. |
| MODERATELY STRONG (STEADY STROKES) | Firm will. Dependable. | Skeptical. Practical. | Disturbed state of mind. |
| STRONG | Assertive sex nature. Moneymaker. | Demanding beneath air of nonchalance. | Insistent but not consistent. Emotional conflict. |
| THICK STROKES | Dominating. Materialistic. Highly sexed. Magnetic. | Tyrannical will that may be concealed. Materialistic. | Shaken confidence and strong conflict of emotion. |
| SPOTTY, SMEARY | Unpredictable temper. Overmaterialistic. | Willful temper. Greed. | Confusion of desires. |
| SHADED DOWNSTROKES | Sensuous. | Sensuous. | Sensuous. Disturbed. |
| SHARP, THIN | Incisive intellect. | Developed critical sense. | Capacity for keenly judging both sides. |

**USE THIS CHART LIKE A TIMETABLE.** You may find more than one type of loop as described in a single writing. Each is significant. Some people are variable and so are their handwritings.

## THE SIGNIFICANCE OF VARIOUS LOOP FORMATIONS

| LOWER LOOPS | RIGHT-SLANTED | VERTICAL OR LEFT-SLANTED |
|---|---|---|
| ROUNDED, COMPLETED | Good vitality. Satisfied sex nature. | More sexy than affectionate. |
| TRIANGULAR | Some self-consciousness regarding sex. Resistant. | Resistant emotions. |
| WEAK, HALF-FINISHED | Immature or ineffectual sex nature. | Fear of sex. |
| EXAGGERATED LENGTH AND WIDTH | Craves luxury, change. Restless nature. | Sex absorption conflicting with fear of sex. Possible complex. |
| BIG, HEAVY-PRESSURED | Strong libido, also a moneymaker. | Materialistic. Magnetic personality. |
| STRAIGHT LINE REPLACES LOWER LOOP | Concentration of thought. Some repression. | Well-concentrated mind. |
| OUTGOING STROKE REPLACES LOWER LOOP | Altruistic, self-sacrificing. | Hidden sympathy for those in need. Secret altruism. |
| TWISTED (CROSSED TWICE) | Sexually uneasy. May punish mate with tyranny. | Fear of opposite sex. |

| UPPER LOOPS | RIGHT-SLANTED | VERTICAL OR LEFT-SLANTED |
|---|---|---|
| WAVED INSTEAD OF LOOPED | Unable to achieve sense of sexual satisfaction. | Unresponsive. |
| HIGH, WIDE | Sensitive, imaginative. | Ambitious, big ideas. |
| TRIANGULAR | Sensitive, touchy. | Sensitive, resistant. |
| HIGH, THIN | Idealistic. | Aloof but craves prestige. |
| STRAIGHT LINE REPLACING LOOP | Direct, alert. | Quick, analytical mind. |
| LOOPS TANGLE WITH LINE ABOVE | Impractical, visionary. | An "escapist" with unreal illusions. |

www.ingramcontent.com/pod-product-compliance
Lightning Source LLC
LaVergne TN
LVHW092324080426
835508LV00039B/528